MARTIN PARR

ONLY HUMAN

ONLY HUMAN

PHOTOGRAPHS BY MARTIN PARR

PHILLIP PRODGER

INTRODUCTION
GRAYSON PERRY

NATIONAL PORTRAIT GALLERY LONDON

CONTENTS

FOREWORD
NICHOLAS CULLINAN

In March 1856, the English aristocrat and politician Philip Henry Stanhope, 5th Earl Stanhope, made a statement to the House of Lords, insisting upon the establishment of a gallery of portraits, 'to consist of those persons who are most honourably commemorated in British history'. The National Portrait Gallery was founded later that year, to document and celebrate the individuals who had contributed to British culture. Today, we remain the only national gallery with a specific focus on British identity, and on the impact and influence of British people who have made their mark on history.

Martin Parr has certainly made his mark. As one of the best-known and most widely celebrated photographers of our time, Martin has cast his wry and satirical gaze on all aspects of modern life. Over a period of fifty years, his photographs have not only documented British society – and beyond – they have also changed the way we look at ourselves, and the way we consider our relationship to the wider world.

Among the many portraits in our collection, we have a photograph of Martin taken in Hebden Bridge, a small town in West Yorkshire where Martin relocated after graduating from Manchester Polytechnic (and, by coincidence, where I grew up). The year is 1974, and in that year, Martin would go on to embark on his first exhibition at Impressions Gallery in York, and to self-publish his first photobook, *Home Sweet Home* (1974). As the photographer Geoff Howard noted, at this point Martin was still working in black and white, rather than the highly saturated colour imagery that he is better known for, and 'he was not a megastar'. Yet. With a camera around his neck and determination in his eyes, the portrait suggests something of the tour de force that Martin would come to be in the world of photography.

Since that year, Martin has participated in thousands of exhibitions and published over one hundred books of his own work, editing around forty more, and his photographs have influenced a new generation of photographers. He has also played an extraordinary role in promoting British photography within the UK and abroad, and in preserving a record of everyday British identity in all its varied guises.

It is fitting, therefore, that we should be recognizing Martin's contribution to contemporary photography by presenting a retrospective of his work. *Only Human* revolves around one of Parr's most important subjects – people. The exhibition that accompanies this book features photographs, taken in the UK and around the world, that reveal the eccentricities of modern life with affection and insight. Martin has keenly observed how we each construct our identities – through the clothes we wear, the people we socialize with or the rituals in which we partake. New work – presented here for the first time – made immediately before and after the Brexit referendum of 2016, in which Britons narrowly voted to leave the European Union, raises complex questions around both national and self-identity. Political developments at home and abroad since that date make these issues particularly pertinent: understanding our national identity is more relevant now than ever. *Only Human* contributes to an ongoing debate about what it means to be British in an international context and reflects on the shared cultural and social history that binds the United Kingdom together during a moment of change.

Dr Nicholas Cullinan, Director
National Portrait Gallery, London

Martin Parr
by Geoff Howard, 1974

PREFACE
PHILLIP PRODGER

In 2014, I ran into Martin Parr at Paris Photo, the trade fair and fashionable art-world event held annually in November. Martin was standing away from the crowds, having a quiet moment at the display of Rose Gallery, his representative in Los Angeles. We had met several times, but Martin did not remember me. I tried to convince him we had, in fact, sat across from each other at dinner once and had a very pleasant conversation. 'You see,' I said, 'I still have your business card in my wallet'. I pulled it out. Looking a bit worse for wear from being inside my wallet for so long, it was not exactly a business card so much as a sticker, the kind of non-descript return address label that companies used to send free with postal promotions. Martin had long used these in place of traditional business cards. 'I've had it for ages,' I explained, 'I just haven't figured out where to stick it yet.' Martin hesitated briefly, considering whether I understood the irony of what I had just said. 'It's no good me talking to you,' Martin replied, 'you're with the National Portrait Gallery. You're only interested in pictures of celebrities, and I only photograph ordinary people. You don't show ordinary people.' I heard this misconception regularly during my time as Head of Photographs at the National Portrait Gallery, and I was eager to dispel it; this seemed like a perfect chance. 'I tell you what,' I answered, 'if you'll agree to show with us, I'll take a proposal back to my committee for an exhibition called *Martin Parr: Ordinary People*. 'OK,' he offered, 'if you take a proposal to your exhibition committee for a show about ordinary people, then I will reveal that I have, in fact, been taking pictures of celebrities for many years, and let you show some of them.' The idea for this book, and the exhibition it accompanies, was born.

The title, 'Ordinary People', did not survive later scrutiny, although a similar phrase remains as the name of a subsection of the project (see p. 40). There was concern that readers might find such a title condescending, as though Martin himself were somehow something other than ordinary. Martin is a gifted artist, photographer, filmmaker, collector, historian and leader in the photographic community, but he would never set himself apart from others in that way. While I agreed with the title change, for me an element of that early title remains the spirit of this book. Through Martin's lens we are *all* ordinary people, and we are all heroic. Whether photographing a stranger, a friend, Her Majesty the Queen or other public figures, Martin approaches each in much the same way. His pictures are often humorous, but the people they portray transcend their comic circumstances.

This book, *Only Human,* picks up where Val Williams' seminal mid-career retrospective of 2002, *Martin Parr,* left off. Although that volume has since been thoughtfully updated, it nevertheless focuses on work made before and during the turn of the millennium. When this project began, the idea was to feature pictures of people from throughout Martin's career, including these earlier pictures, but it quickly became apparent that the quality of Martin's output is so consistent, and his production so voluminous, that narrowing the selection would result in a stronger project.

Moreover, a lot has happened since 2002. The political and economic situation in the United Kingdom continues to evolve, so much so that pictures which once seemed bitterly satirical, such as those of New Brighton in Merseyside during the Thatcher years, published as *The Last Resort* (1986), now seem gentler and less acerbic. Martin's interests have become more international, while Britain has arguably grown more insular, famously voting by plebiscite in 2016 to exit the European Union. As his fame has grown, Martin has also gained access to people and places to which the public are not freely admitted, a subject he calls 'The Establishment', which has become an important part of his recent work. And in his own practice, he has increasingly embraced the role of curator and cultural custodian, becoming president of the legendary agency Magnum from 2013–7, and opening the Martin Parr Foundation in 2017. Combined, these factors suggest there is much new to discuss.

Concentrating largely on work made since 2002 has also had two positive but unintended consequences. First, it has shown that, while Martin's interests have been remarkably consistent over the course of his career, he has never followed a fixed formula. The public associate him with several techniques which he may or may not employ depending on the circumstances – fill flash, photographing in close-up with a macro lens and printing in saturated colour. While all of these elements do still feature (flash, in particular, remains a signature), they are only arrows in his quiver, to be drawn as needed. Visually, his work is more complex than ever, as he constantly tests new ways of making pictures. Recently, for example, he began using a telephoto lens to photograph from long distances at the beach. This not only enables him to photograph completely unobserved, but also to explore new ways of graphically organizing space.

The second unintended consequence is historical. For nearly half a century, Martin has been our eyes (and ears) during a time of technological, scientific, cultural and economic upheaval. Since the early 1970s when he began photographing, Britain – and indeed the entire world – has changed. Focusing on the last 15–20 years of work has provided a once-in-a-generation view of the impact of globalization, migration, consumerism and the leisure industry at

a time of political volatility. When I ran into Martin in Paris in 2014, Scotland had just narrowly voted to remain in the UK during the Scottish independence referendum. Neither of us had any idea that one year later (almost to the day) and during the same Paris art fair, terrorists would brutally attack the Stade de France and the Bataclan theatre just a few kilometres away. Nor could we have imagined that the UK would narrowly vote to leave the European Union just a year after that. We could not have anticipated the rise of far-right extremism in the United States and certain segments of the population in Europe, including the UK. And yet these things did happen, and Martin has been photographing all the while. He has been like a psychologist with a difficult patient, a camera for a clipboard, reserving his diagnosis, but monitoring our symptoms.

INTRODUCTION
GRAYSON PERRY

Whether we are aware of it or not, we are all scanning culture continuously for things that validate us; experiences that chime with how we already feel and reinforce who we think we are.

When I first came upon the photography of Martin Parr in a colour supplement at some point in the 1980s, a very loud bell rang. Here was someone who was pointing out with laser precision the aspects of society I didn't even know I was driven by. He framed anthropological observations that I didn't yet know I was fascinated by. Class, identity, individualism and belonging, what it is to be British: in these subjects, Martin's photos are my guiding text. Often the most affecting encounters with culture are those that make concrete the wisps of feeling we have been sensing for years. For me, the photographs of Martin Parr did just that, and I'm sure they have done the same thing for millions of other people all over the planet.

Since that first encounter, his work has been a guiding beacon for me, pointing out patterns and dissonances in society, but more importantly showing me *how* to look. Over the course of his long and vastly prolific career – to date he has produced more than 100 books and many more exhibitions – Martin has developed an anthropological 'sat nav' that will reliably take him to where his hyper-developed image-making skills can play and disrupt. His genius is not just in spotting the shot, but in booking the flight and getting the access.

Perhaps what I sensed in those photographs from the off was an ambivalence about the subjects that I shared. I look at those images of county ladies stuffing their faces, tourists trapped in clichés, ridiculous fanatics, drunken revellers and the jolly grim British working classes, and they all seem to be hovering uncomfortably between comedy and tragedy. Humour

bleeds through all these photographs, but also compassion. 'How dare you take yourself seriously?' they say, but then 'Let's celebrate that impulse' – in a quietly bonkers, British way, naturally.

Martin's British sensibility is one reason I feel it a shame that he, though of course hugely respected in his home country, is much more of a cultural celebrity in France. His photographs are beautiful and deserve to be hung alongside the Bechers, Brandts and Gurskys that have infiltrated the art galleries. Perhaps humour is not taken seriously by the gatekeepers of 'high' culture. Perhaps we are discomforted – embarrassed, even – by what he shows us of ourselves. He is, after all, an equal opportunities satirist, and the art world itself has not been spared. This book and the show it accompanies will, I hope, recruit many more admirers of what I think of as our most exquisitely British eye.

Martin himself is, of course, just like one of his own impassioned and ridiculous fanatics. At any one time, he might have half a dozen bids pending on eBay for a Martin Luther King lamp, a Soviet space-dog thermometer or a Saddam Hussein watch that he hopes to add to his world-class collection of postcards, tea trays and political ephemera. All photographers are to some extent collectors, but Martin has taken this to a meta level in amassing one of the largest collections of photobooks in the world. He is a profound expert on photography, as well as one of its most influential advocates.

And what of Martin Parr the man? I first met him at a party about fifteen years ago. I was very drunk and went up and hugged him, and said, 'I love you'. A cliché worthy of his scrutiny, perhaps, despite which we struck up a friendship. Getting to know him, it was no surprise to find him not only very funny but also an assiduous student of comedy, who makes an effort to see as many live shows as he can. He is also generous, not just in his championing of other photographers but also in his support for institutions of which he approves through his work. He is also the hardest-working person I know, forever on the move, clocking up enough air miles to take him and his wife Susie on a first-class, round-the-world tour. That in itself is very characteristic, as Martin has a gimlet eye for a bargain and sometimes berates me for my (relatively) sloppy attitude to money.

One of the first things I asked him is something I'm sure other people must wonder: 'How do you get away with taking some of these photographs?' If I saw Martin striding purposefully towards me with a camera, I would be tempted to run. The few times he has taken my photo, I have ended up looking like someone in a Martin Parr photograph. I stare blankly out, my pretentions pinned like a butterfly to a card. I have occasionally seen him at work in the field, alert but camouflaged by banality. He has developed a carefully crafted image: the genial dowdy everyman that no one will notice, in faded clothes and sandals, who pokes the camera in someone's face with utter confidence and then turns away and disappears into the background the split second after pressing the shutter.

Like all great artists, Martin Parr has altered how we see the world. We see a queue of posh people, a buffet served on a Union Jack tablecloth or a lurid beach scene and we think of his work. He is one of the foremost chroniclers of our times. He sees our tender aspirations, our vanities, our sincere enthusiasms, our anachronistic traditions, our often unpredictable diversity – and he both ribs us and applauds us, blinded by his flash and decked in saturated colour.

Martin, Martin

When will you be starting
A serious career in photography?
Passports, weddings, baskets full of kittens
Martin, your attitude baffles and it sickens!

Once I asked Martin to take some pics of me
Relaxing at home with my loving family
With hands like 'so', but Martin said 'No'
And proceeded to snap a plate of mashed potato!

Martin, Martin
When will you be starting
A serious career in photography?
Passports, weddings, baskets full of kittens
Martin, your attitude baffles and it sickens!

Well, I told Martin how to take a photograph
You say 'Watch the birdie!' and try to make them laugh
Or at least smile … Martin meanwhile
Was focusing his lens on a nearby rubbish pile!

And when will this silliness stop?
Photos of light switches, lampshades, the lot
Pleasing to the eye it is not!
And when for goodness' sake will he open a shop?

Martin, Martin
When will you be starting
A serious career in photography?
Passports, weddings, baskets full of kittens
Martin, your attitude baffles and it sickens!

(Optional lines – sung on the occasion of Martin's
sixtieth birthday)
What a strange chap you are!
But nevertheless, happy birthday, Martin Parr!

– JOHN SHUTTLEWORTH

Autoportrait, Honey Rose Studio,
Mexico City, Mexico, 2008

Autoportrait, Yalta,
Russia, 2008

Autoportrait, Dubai,
United Arab Emirates, 2007

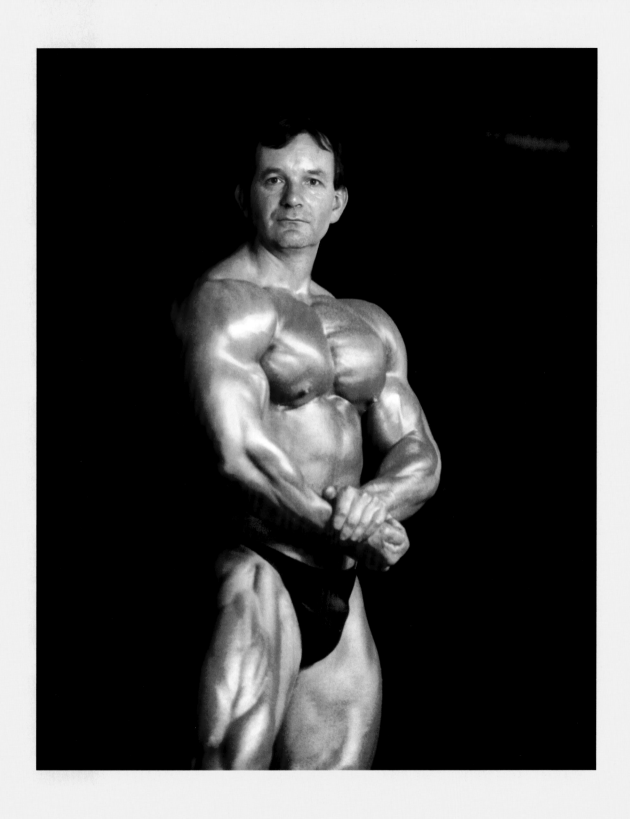

Autoportrait, New York,
USA, 1999

Studio de la Tour Eiffel - Paris

Autoportrait, Studio de la Tour Eiffel,
Paris, France, 1999

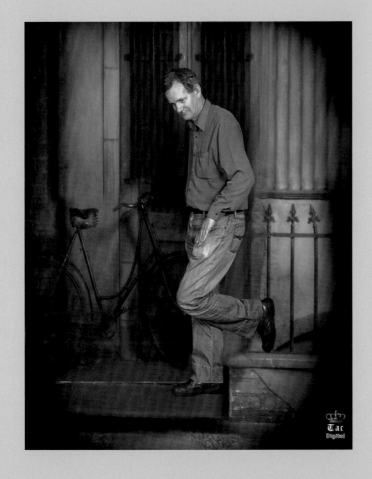

Autoportrait, Donalds Studio,
Colombo, Sri Lanka, 2003

Autoportrait, Tac Digital Photo Studio,
London, England, 2008

Autoportrait, Fortaleza,
Brazil, 2008

AUTOPORTRAIT OF AN ISLAND HOPPER

JOACHIM SCHMID

One of the things that puzzles me time and again when we talk about photography is the use of the singular. 'Photography' – as if a photo booth machine in a bustling Paris Metro station has anything to do with an old man who takes an occasional snapshot at a remote place close to the end of the world. That's like asking what a poet, an accountant and a judge signing a death sentence have in common. They all use writing implements, it's true – but that doesn't tell us anything about the peculiar activities of any of the three.

The singular 'photography' suggests one cohesive field, something like a continent. Everyone will admit that there are a number of different regions with their specific particularities in this continent – art, fashion, journalism and so on. But if you take a closer look, it's probably an archipelago rather than a continent, and the number of tiny islands have not even been counted yet. The inhabitants of one island have little or nothing to do with those of another, and what is known to be true on one island may be completely unknown and irrelevant on another one. Life is comfortable that way; you don't have to ask too many questions and can avoid a war or two.

So let's talk about the plural – 'photographies'. The word subsumes diverse practices, and many of the practitioners have little or no knowledge of or interest in the work done on other islands. Some of them even deny the existence of other islands. There are exceptions, however, and Martin Parr is one of them. He has worked on all the islands mentioned above, and as an avid island hopper has visited quite a number of remote areas. Probably the clearest demonstration of this quirk is his collection of autoportraits.

Don't expect a photographer looking at a mirror, though, camera in hand. Autoportrait in this case means that the photographer submitted himself to all available portrait procedures offered by anyone anywhere in the world, no matter how tacky or atrocious they may seem to the educated mind. Yes, that's photography, and it's one of the legitimate islands where people make a living by using a camera. These photographers may have their aesthetic preferences and their professional pride, but at the end of the day it's a job done for the money they count after closing the shop.

Exploring this island is a job for brave men; I know that from personal experience. Before I saw Martin's portraits, I had been doing the same for some years, or let's say nearly the same. I gave up on my endeavour when I learned about his, not because someone else had done it but because I noticed two mistakes I had made. First mistake: I was too stingy. In my little corner of the world you simply don't spend money on something that's unquestionably rubbish. Second mistake: looking at Martin's collection I understood that you have to be absolutely free of any vanity, and I realized I am not. To create a compelling collection, you have to be willing to collaborate with a photographer who makes you look like a complete idiot; knowing you'll look like an idiot, you must be ready to hand over cash to that person, preferably with a smile on your face.

Talking of smiles, maybe you have noticed the lack thereof in the portraits themselves. The no-smile principle seems to be a conceptual no-brainer, but resisting the photographers' expert attempts to seduce the client is something that has to be mastered. Martin is good at it. Leafing through his book, I was reminded of my own failures and of situations when I said no to a portrait opportunity. Nobody wants to look like an idiot, but sometimes it has to be done.

So what do autoportraits not made by the photographer tell us about the subject's self? Not much, really. Just like all commercially motivated portraits, they tell us more about the photographers' methods of glossing over and commodifying their sitter than about the often carefully preserved identity of the person depicted. As a series, however, they highlight one aspect of the personality, which is Martin's virtually unlimited curiosity for all things photographic. While most of us may have encountered and experienced a few of these savage photo opportunities, he has accepted them all, without declining even the most ridiculous. With no fear of contact, he got all the pictures made as a representative for the universal traveller who is welcome everywhere – as long as there's some cash to be gained. Without Martin's autoportraits, there would be more blank spots in that unmapped area of photographies. And a bonus for the anxious and vain parts of the audience: you can enjoy the imagery without looking like an idiot yourself.

Joachim Schmid, Tiznit,
Morocco, 1987

Autoportrait, Nairobi,
Kenya, 2010

Autoportrait, Riga,
Latvia, 1999

This page and opposite:
Fotoescultura, hand-painted photograph on metal,
with wood carving by Bruno Eslava, 2009

Autoportrait with Lionel Messi,
Barcelona, Spain, 2012

Autoportrait, Dubai, United
Arab Emirates, 2009

Online dating profile picture,
Hey Saturday, London, England, 2016

WHO DO YOU THINK YOU ARE?

There is a famous passage in Chuck Palahniuk's dystopian novel *Fight Club* (1996) in which a gas explosion tears through the narrator's fifteenth-floor flat, destroying everything he owns. Seeing all his possessions reduced to ash and scattered on the ground below, he reflects on their destruction and the excitement he once felt selecting each item from the Ikea catalogue:

> The Alle cutlery service. Stainless steel. Dishwasher safe.
> The Vild hall clock made of galvanized steel, oh, I had to have that.
> The Klipsk shelving unit, oh, yeah.
> Hemlig hat boxes. Yes.
> [...] It took my whole life to buy this stuff.
> The easy-care textured lacquer of my Kalix occasional tables.
> My Steg nesting tables.
> You buy furniture. You tell yourself, this is the last sofa I will ever need in my life. Buy the sofa, then for a couple years you're satisfied that no matter what else goes wrong, at least you've got your sofa issue handled. Then the right set of dishes. Then the perfect bed. The drapes. The rug. Then you're trapped in your lovely nest, and the things you used to own, now they own you.[1]

Faced with the wholesale loss of these once-cherished items, the narrator realizes the folly of shopping as a means of self-improvement. At the same time, he comes to understand that his purchases have taken on an unexpected psychological dimension. His furnishings are no longer just useful objects: they have become an extension of his personality, or at least of whom he perceives himself to be. Well-made, practical and stylish, they are self-anointed emblems of his character, carefully chosen to reassure himself and impress others. But how much of this was really him, and how much had he merely succumbed to effective merchandising? And if the latter, what did that say about him, anyway?

Martin Parr excels at portraying the many external elements that surround and define us. Not just the things we buy, but the clothes we wear, the sports teams we champion, the clubs and political parties to which we belong and the traditions we honour. Do we wave the Cross of St George or St Andrew? Are we Brexiteers or Remainers? Do we go barefoot on the beach or wear white socks with sandals? What do our homes look like, our dining tables and our teacakes? The people Parr photographs are surrounded by evidence of the choices they have made.

To those unacquainted with his photography, the world Parr portrays may seem unsettling. Through his lens, the resplendent artificiality of contemporary consumer culture seems to vibrate with energy. Tinsel, icing, neon, bunting and fairy lights glow in hyper-saturated hues, while textiles flatten into broad, bold expanses of colour. The people and places he photographs are frequently improvised and disarranged by the people who inhabit them; they may appear riotous, cacophonous, garish or nonsensical. If the colours seem unreal, it is because they are resolutely synthetic, plastic and polymerized, printed in glossy advertisements and emblazoned on paper cups. Parr makes no attempt to obscure their manufactured character. Frequently photographed with flash, his subjects are plainly laid bare, denied even the modesty of shadow. Sometimes positioning himself at oblique angles, and cutting off the edge of

'Identity itself is a complex and elusive subject. In the museum of our minds we may think of ourselves one way, but we are not always the most reliable judges of our own character.'

the frame in unexpected places, Parr allows blur and extremes of focus to enter his pictures. The results may appear haphazard, yet their success hinges on small, acutely observed details.

Questions of identity and self are among the most enduring in photographic practice. Traditionally, portraiture has been viewed as a reductionist exercise, a paring down of information to arrive at the essential elements of personality. Consequently, the job of the portraitist has been to strip away extraneous information to arrive at a sitter's genuine self. This somewhat romantic approach is based on the belief that while who we are is ultimately mysterious and unknowable, a glimmer of understanding may be achieved through a mediated encounter; that while true identity is fundamentally elusive, people nevertheless betray inner thoughts and feelings through their revealing gestures and expressions. The skilful portraitist makes these moments visible to the viewer. Much studio portraiture subscribes to this model, in which the photographer becomes guide and the picture a substitute for face-to-face meeting. In the right hands, such pictures can be extraordinarily effective. The best offer insight into the life of the sitter, the photographer and sometimes even the viewer. However, such photographs are not without problems, since what the camera is able to capture is limited and there are many different ways of thinking about self. And there are other ways of triangulating on personality, as Parr demonstrates.

Identity itself is a complex and elusive subject. In the museum of our minds we may think of ourselves one way, but we are not always the most reliable judges of our own character. We may also aspire to be something other than what we think we are, a 'true self' that may or may not ever materialize. Our families will have one view of us, our co-workers another and so on. Moreover, personalities are by nature fluid, subject to change and adaptation. An adult may display some of the same qualities as he or she did as a child, but each of us is learning and evolving every day. The way we behave also depends on circumstances. Under pressure, we may act one way, relaxed another. We have public and private personas, conscious and unconscious behaviours. And we may seek to hide the darker sides of our inner selves – our selfishness and irascibility, insecurities and petty grievances. Ultimately, the myriad of qualities that distinguish us from others is cumulative and ephemeral and, strictly speaking, unphotographable.

In traditional portraits, the objects and manner of dress that appear in a picture may be purposely arranged to reflect notable aspects of the sitter's personality. Thus, a vicar might appear holding a bible or a book of hymns, a judge might carry a gavel or an author might hold a pen. Such conceits may seem quaint in a consumer culture in which branding is paramount. This is an area which Parr's colleague, the Dutch artist Hans Eijkelboom, has explored since 1992 with his project *People of the Twenty-First Century*. Working in two-hour sessions, Eijkelboom photographs people he sees on the street who have made parallel decisions of style or taste, before making the images into grids. In *Photo Note August 19th*, for example, he found a dozen men in Amsterdam wearing T-shirts decorated with John Pasche's famous 'tongue' logo for The Rolling Stones (fig. 1). Eijkelboom's works point to one of the paradoxes of mass-produced goods: although they may be chosen to reflect our unique personalities, it is likely many others will have them, too.

If Eijkelboom shows us our plumage, Parr exposes our feathers, feeding habits and nesting grounds. He describes himself as a 'social documentary' photographer, associating with a tradition of picture-making historically identified with movements for political and socioeconomic improvement. This may surprise those who view his photographs primarily as mischievous entertainment, since it suggests a sincere wish on the part of the photographer to affect social change. Yet Parr's photographs frequently transcend the apparent triviality of the circumstances they depict.

Parr wears the term 'social documentary' like an ill-fitting suit, although this is arguably because the label itself deserves reappraisal. Increasingly in recent years, the term 'social documentary' has been challenged, since the words 'social' and 'documentary' are both potentially contentious. Because portraits cost both money and time, their 'social' point of view has been regarded as one of privilege; particularly in the past, this has meant that marginalized groups have not been adequately represented. The word 'documentary' is additionally fraught, as it suggests a photographer observing the world with rigorous objective detachment, which is seldom desirable and arguably impossible to achieve. All photographers have an attitude towards the things they photograph, even when the results look comparatively neutral.

Nevertheless, the phrase is still useful for an artist who is otherwise hard to pigeonhole. In his daily practice, Parr is both a fine-art and a commercial photographer, exhibiting and selling prints through galleries while at the same time accepting commissions for editorial, fashion and, less frequently, advertising work. His images are also marketed through the Magnum agency, where he is a strong presence, having served as the organization's president from 2013–17. In reality, there is little meaningful distinction to be made between these various categories, since in most cases work made for commercial purposes can be repurposed as exhibition pieces, and vice versa. 'I am a firm believer in high and low culture and photography working together,' Parr explains.[2]

Parr is not usually thought of as a traditional portraitist, although a number of the photographs in this book – notably in the 'Autoportrait' and 'Celebrity' sections (pp. 13–23, 68–87) – approach a conventional definition of portraiture. However, such pictures represent only a small fraction of his output. Most of his pictures of people are what might be called 'environmental portraits', images in which identity of person and place intertwine. Time and again, people are shown in circumstances that provide a window, however small, on their personality. Norman Soper, for example, the garden enthusiast who won 'Best Pot Leek' at the Sandwell Show in 2010, stands with his prize-winning entry neatly aligned with his torso, its luxurious leaves seeming almost to emanate from his heart, marked with a red ribbon (p. 42). Facing the camera squarely and with his feet firmly planted, he extends his arms towards the viewer, cradling the vegetable like a supplicant making an offering. Or Evelyn Marie Seidel, member of the Lady Di Club in Hamelin, Germany, where the British Army had a presence until 2014 (p. 47), stands partially behind a life-sized cardboard photo of the princess. Ms Seidel's lavender hat echoes the princess's sash. Diana also appears on her handbag, a cock-eyed Union Jack perched behind it, her right forearm and bare neck exposing pearl that resemble the ones Diana frequently wore. In another photograph, a boy and girl

'[Parr] takes us behind the scenes, revealing us as we never intended to be seen, our actions unrehearsed and unpolished, our facial expressions awkward. Such times are representative of our daily selves and of the web of decisions that shape and snare us.'

sit on a roadside eating watermelon, the boy holding a green dinosaur balloon, the girl a unicorn (p. 165). The curious parallel between the matching colours of the boy's balloon and the green hair of the woman behind him, and the 'T-Rex' T-shirt worn by the man to his left, belies their physical separation.

At the racecourse, women choose feathered hats and fascinators to match their vibrant dresses and sunglasses, while men wear bowlers and top hats (pp. 120–131). Every visitor to the beach displays her or his own distinctive towel and swimsuit, carefully chosen. Dozens of surfers on the beach at St Ives carry a variety of surfboards, each slightly different in shape, colour and decoration (p. 223). In Britain, questions of social status often sneak into the frame, as when an immaculately dressed official with a Burberry-style jacket and high heels looks on in scrutiny at the Lincolnshire Show, standing unwittingly next to a sign reading 'Class Judging, 1st, 2nd' (p. 178).

When the legendary French photographer Henri Cartier-Bresson wrote to Parr in 1995 protesting that Parr's works were 'from another planet',[3] it was arguably pictures like these which provoked him. Parr rarely shows us a 'decisive moment', as Cartier-Bresson had it – the photograph as stage, in which everything resolves into meaningful synchronicity for a flicker of an instant. Instead, he takes us behind the scenes, revealing us as we never intended to be seen, our actions unrehearsed and unpolished, our facial expressions awkward. Such times are representative of our daily selves and of the web of decisions that shape and snare us. Parr's world is experiential, exaggerated and fragmentary, its visual logic inscrutable. Aesthetically, Cartier-Bresson may as well have lived on another planet.

Other factors contributed to Cartier-Bresson's bafflement, as photographers including Parr began to rethink the role of photography in the late twentieth century. Cartier-Bresson was one of a number of highly influential photographers for whom the experience of the Second World War (Cartier-Bresson himself spent nearly three years in a German prison camp) created a sense a moral obligation to use photography as a constructive political tool, highlighting injustice and facilitating understanding between peoples. This so-called 'humanist' impulse was among the driving factors in the creation of Magnum Photos, which included Cartier-Bresson, Robert Capa, David Seymour (known as 'Chim') and George Rodger among its founders.

Two generations later, Parr's decision to apply for full membership at Magnum created controversy within the organization, as some believed his photography to be inconsistent with the founders' legacy. In June 1994, during the Magnum annual general meeting at which Parr was to be elevated to full member, the matter came to a head, with photographer Philip Jones Griffiths leading the opposition. In a famously splenetic letter, Jones Griffiths accused Parr of failing to uphold the founder's values:

Martin Parr ... is an unusual photographer in the sense that he has always shunned the values that Magnum was built on. Not for him any of our concerned 'finger on the pulse of society' humanistic photography ... Today he wants to be a member. The vote will be a declaration of who we are and a statement of how we see ourselves. His membership would not be a proclamation of diversity but the rejection of those values that have given Magnum the status it has in the world today ... Let me state that I have great respect for him as the dedicated enemy of everything I believe in and, I trust, what Magnum still believes in.[4]

Parr prevailed by the narrowest of margins, but Jones Griffiths had identified a growing tension not only within Magnum, but within the photographic community more broadly. Those photographers who clung to the vision of the medium as an instrument of social justice were alarmed by the equivocation they perceived in the younger generation, including Parr. Yet these artists emerged at a time when right and wrong were not always so pronounced as they had been during a time of war, and the mundane experience of daily life was once again open to exploration and question. It was not that the photographers themselves were ambiguous in their beliefs, only that the circumstances were complex and open-ended in a way that previous generations had not seen.

Photographers of Cartier-Bresson's generation recognized the dramatic changes wrought by the Second World War, but could not have anticipated the scale of the transformation that would follow. In 1949, the American photographer Max Yavno's photograph *Muscle Beach, Los Angeles* was considered an extreme of visual chaos (fig. 2). The storefronts and sidings advertising food, drink and gymnastic training ('modern, clean, safe'); women climbing on men's backs, scaling equipment and flying through the air; the upper storey of a row of houses in the background: all signify a kind of cultural anarchy, of letting loose old constraints. Unusually for the time, advertising is also an integral part of the scene. A Coca-Cola sign presides over the beach in the upper left, while a young couple, their backs to the camera, look on. Some sixty-five years later, Parr's *Grandé Beach Mar Del Plata, Argentina* reveals how much has changed since Yavno's time (pp. 220–221). Coca-Cola still has pride of place, its distinctive red and white logo – little changed from the 1940s – looking on from bottom centre, and from scattered deck chairs and beach umbrellas. The sand itself is nearly standing-room-only, and a queue snakes towards the snack bar, across the centre of the frame. Dense and horizonless, and in Parr's hands now searing with colour, it shows a world Yavno could scarcely have recognized. Overstuffed and constraining – still anarchic, but no longer free. A visit to the beach no longer seems so welcoming.

Spurred on by international political and economic policies prioritizing growth, the late twentieth and early twenty-first centuries have witnessed unprecedented levels of material abundance. Andreas Gursky's celebrated turn-of-the-millennium composition *99 Cent* is one of the best-known artistic representations of this dramatic change. It shows the interior of an American 99-cent store, in which everything costs less than a dollar (fig. 3). In Gursky's photograph, shoppers meander through the aisles, unfazed but passive, eyeing the varieties of sweets, biscuits and fizzy drinks that fill the shelves to the point of collapse. Each product competes for the shoppers' attention, with showy graphics and flashy colours – lemon yellows, candy pinks and sky blues – to attract buyers like bees to flowers. Behind each packet sit dozens more, ready to take the place of any purchases. The profusion of cheap, available *stuff* is overwhelming, the role of the individual in such an environment unclear. Is such a place empowering, dehumanizing or both?

When Parr tackles similar subject matter, the emphasis becomes more personal. A woman in a pink sweat suit top and skinny jeans pushes a wheeled shopping trolley, talking on a mobile phone while she fiddles with her handbag (p. 153). As she speaks, she leans forwards slightly, revealing the dark roots of her dyed blonde hair. The shop she has just left – Stack it High, Sell it Cheap! – invades the pavement around her with pallet upon pallet of diet cola and fruit squash, stacked, true to its name, waist deep, the prices – £1 or £1.50 – handwritten in Sharpie on strips of cardboard and loose sheets of A4. If Gursky presents a kind of sterile corporate fantasy of economic success, Parr shows us the individual swept up within its reality.

Shopping and selling are recurring themes in Parr's work. In his hometown of Bristol he shows a meticulously presented car boot sale, a mother and two children beside a bright blue Ford Fiesta hatchback, parked against a graffitied concrete wall (p. 172). The car is shiny and well looked-after, and the items for sale are artfully arranged. Nothing touches the ground: two pairs of shoes sit on a car mat, while a neatly ordered collection of books and girls' clothing sits on a blue blanket. A smaller blanket holds toys, including a monster truck, a bulldozer and a robot. The girl sits on a stool studying an iPad, while her brother attempts to climb on the car windscreen. The picture serves both as a record of the sale and a portrait of the family – a window on their values and relationships, how they dress and how they play.

In another photograph, a grey-haired woman sits alone in a shopping centre, retreating into the corner of a red vinyl sofa (p. 152). Her hair neatly set, her shoulders close and knees together, she holds one gloved hand in another, presumably sheltering from the cold. She eyes the camera suspiciously, whilst with a characteristic sense of irony, Parr captures both the woman and the rubbish bin behind her, decorated with an ad for Floradix tonic. 'Tired of being Tired?' the ad reads, a model yawning widely to illustrate the question: it is as if the ad has been made to manifest the shopper's inner thoughts.

Shopping centres have been a mainstay of Parr's photography for much of his career. In 2002, he orchestrated a series of works at The Mall at Cribbs Causeway in Bristol, showing shoppers standing with shopping bags bulging with purchases, spindly decorative indoor palms visible in the background (fig. 4). These photographs are unusual in that Parr asked the sitters to stop and pose; ordinarily, he photographs more surreptitiously. The resulting 'shopping portraits' show Parr's interest in teasing apart the connections between consumer culture and identity.

The human capacity to invest material objects with personal meaning is a phenomenon the business theorist Russell Belk has famously described as 'the extended self'.[5] Writing in the late 1980s, Belk argued that humans have a complex relationship with the things with which we choose to surround ourselves. When we buy furniture, clothing or cutlery of a certain style, we send signals about our social status, preferences and beliefs. And yet on a psychological level, those same things unconsciously may become part of how we perceive ourselves. 'We are what we have,' Belk concluded.[6]

Ironically, when Belk developed his theory of the extended self, he did so in the context of improving sales and marketing strategies. He hoped that better

'Comedy exists where expectations
are defeated, and there is a poignancy
bordering on melancholy that
emerges from much of his work.'

understanding of the psychology behind consumer behaviour would help businesses to target consumers more effectively. For Belk, this was by no means a bad thing. In the 1960s and 1970s, many scholars still accepted the analysis of Karl Marx, who had argued a century earlier that consumption provides a false path to happiness through what he described as 'commodity fetishism'. A sceptic he may have been, but Marx nevertheless recognized the complex and devoted relationships people may have with their belongings. 'A commodity appears, at first sight, a very trivial thing,' he wrote, 'and easily understood. Its analysis shows us that it is, in reality, a very queer thing, abounding in metaphysical subtleties and theological niceties.'[7]

By the 1980s, spurred by increasing globalization, many people had begun to question if consumerism could produce lasting happiness. Belk, though, was of the view that consumption could lead to greater self-esteem and overall satisfaction with life. According to him, '[We] use material possessions to seek happiness, remind ourselves of experiences, accomplishments and other people in our lives, and even create a sense of immortality after death. Our accumulation of possessions provides a sense of past and tells us who we are, where we have come from, and perhaps where we are going.'[8]

Photographers have not always been so sanguine. In 1986, just two years before Belk published his essay, the American photographer Lee Friedlander produced an influential series of photographs of people working at the Cray Electronics facility in Chippewa Falls, Wisconsin (fig. 5). Although not focused on possessions per se, it explored the question of human relationships with equipment

in the workplace. Friedlander's photographs show people interacting with supercomputers and other machines, some of which had reached such inordinate complexity as to be scarcely comprehensible to all but a handful of specialists. He showed employees lost in concentration, hunched over their machines, preoccupied with minutiae. The relationship he revealed was not one-dimensional but symbiotic, with humans existing to serve the machine as much as the machine served them. Rather than objects as extensions of people, he showed people as extensions of objects.

This spirit of ambiguity pervades Martin Parr's photography, as it is often unclear whether an individual controls his or her own circumstances or the circumstances control them. The actor who portrays the relentlessly cheerful bingo mascot Mecca Rebecca, for example, removes her costume head to smoke a cigarette, her own put-upon expression the antithesis of the character's, her body slumped backwards and her legs splayed out as far as the costume permits (p. 44). The tennis player Rafael Nadal signs autographs as a tidal wave of well-wishing fans push and grapple for his attention while taking pictures of him on their mobile phones (pp. 118–119). An unnamed English patriot, a St George's flag draped around his neck, watches children play on an inflatable Mickey Mouse bouncy slide, his body aligned with a pink dividing wall so that he looks like nothing so much as an extension of Mickey's nose (p. 159).

Martin Parr has been accused of ridiculing the people he photographs, yet the humour in his photographs never comes at others' expense. Comedy exists where expectations are defeated, and there is a poignancy

'As viewers, we admire people as focused and passionate as these. If only we, too, could cast aside our inhibitions and live in the moment, unselfconsciously and seemingly without care.'

bordering on melancholy that emerges from much of his work.

Parr is on our side even when the cards are stacked against us. Humans are eccentric by nature, but they are also resilient and adaptable. If it is a nice day, what harm is there in casting aside one's suitcase and lying on the beach (p. 219)? Or reclining like the Rokeby Venus on hard cobblestones, discreetly hiding one's tummy with a shopping bag (p. 218)? Parr may allow himself a smile over such petty social infractions, but he treats his subjects with admiration, quietly cheering them on when, celebrating Pride in a wheelchair on a hot summer's day, a woman garlands her head with flowers, raises her hands in the air as far as she can and belts out a song (p. 101). Or, when the temperature at the Australian Open exceeds 40 °C, another woman throws herself at cooling fans in a backwards dive, yelping with delight (p. 115). Who cares if anyone is watching? As viewers, we admire people as focused and passionate as these. If only we, too, could cast aside our inhibitions and live in the moment, unselfconsciously and seemingly without care.

One of Parr's best-known photographs from the 1980s depicts two children eating ice creams on the promenade in New Brighton, Merseyside (fig. 6). The children, an older boy and younger girl dressed in blue recall Gainsborough's painting *Blue Boy* (1779), stand side by side, clutching cones of rapidly melting vanilla whip, the drips flowing over hands and wrists, dropping onto their bare shins and splattering on the curb. The girl looks directly at the camera, a stuffed Mr Men toy dangling from one arm, her mouth ringed clown-like with ice cream. The boy's shirt is a souvenir from New Orleans, with the slogan 'Dynamite Comes in Small Packages' printed on the front. He looks away

into the distance, a stoic expression on his face, ice cream painted from cheek to chin and a large drop dribbling from his jaw.

The picture appeared in the series *The Last Resort,* first published in 1986 and now in its fifth edition. New Brighton was developed in the mid-nineteenth century as a seaside resort, mainly serving the city of Liverpool and nearby communities in North West England. At the time of its creation, its namesake, Brighton in East Sussex, was a thriving and established resort in the south, so the name 'New Brighton' was aspirational. By 1986 the original Brighton had declined significantly, so the idea that a community might aim to be a 'new' version of another rundown seaside town was itself ironic. The overall health of the British leisure industry notwithstanding, New Brighton was in a particularly tired state. Parr's photographs show a shoreline strewn with rubbish, one-armed bandits lit with bare fluorescent tubes, broken glass and long-neglected, rusted Victorian architecture. As photo historian Gerry Badger recalls, a reviewer in the *British Journal of Photography* described the scene in virtually post-apocalyptic terms, as '... a clammy, claustrophobic nightmare world where people lie knee-deep in chip papers, swim in polluted black pools and stare at the bleak horizon of urban dereliction'.[9]

Badger goes on to explain that the circumstances in New Brighton were not as bad as they appeared. Scruffy, yes, and overburdened with use, but not abandoned. To be fair, several of Parr's photographs in *The Last Resort* show cranes and bulldozers deployed to shore up the sea wall and repair boat ramps and pavements, and the New Brighton Lido, as Badger points out, was in a decent condition.[10]

Still, Parr's project generated controversy. Some interpreted pictures such as the children eating ice cream as thinly veiled criticism of Thatcherite policies, which privileged middle-class enclaves over working-class haunts such as New Brighton. Others imagined Parr as a culture snob, sneering at the working classes.

The picture taps into several persistent themes of Parr's work. The ice creams may be disintegrating in the children's hands, yet the children are undeterred. One senses they could not enjoy them more were they in the finest Italian *gelateria*. When the promise of an intact ice cream meets the reality of a melted one, the children do not dwell on the loss – they make the best of it. Their imaginations allow them to see past disappointment and prize what they enjoy. Throughout *The Last Resort,* Parr uncovers ingenuity in the face of imperfect circumstances. A woman sunbathes on a concrete incline perilously close to the vicious treads of a parked digger. A man creates a makeshift sunshade by propping up the bonnet of his Skoda. A couple shelter from the rain by folding beach chairs over their heads. A naked boy makes a game out of crossing a crumbled retaining wall and a shoreline spread with litter, while his mother looks on attentively, holding his trousers. The point is not that these circumstances are seedy or degraded, but that people transcend them. Unperturbed, they see past the chipped paint, sunken walkways and faded signs. They soak up the sun, walk their dogs and play with their children.

In the 1990s, Parr's most persistent critic was arguably former *Economist, Independent Magazine* and *Reportage* picture editor, Colin Jacobson. In a 1996 article, Jacobson seized on the example of a Parr photograph of a Conservative Party summer fete as particularly cruel:

> Do we laugh at the odd way in which these people stand, or dress, or look? Or do we delve further in the value-systems we attribute to these individuals? Surely, they are mealy-mouthed, narrow-minded little-Englanders? ... The fact is, neither we nor Parr know anything about these individuals, other than they were attending a Tory garden party. They are, therefore, being used as props in a photographic sideshow; the pictures invite us to throw sponges at the cardboard cut-outs. It would be disconcerting for Parr if he were to discover that these individuals were actually rather kind and caring, and did not believe that criminals should be flogged in public. As a photographer, he cannot afford to know anything about them as people, because this would upset his attitudinal apple cart.[11]

Jacobson criticized Parr for dissociating himself emotionally from the subject, yet photography is by definition dissociative. There is nothing about the photograph that indicates Parr did not know the individuals to be 'kind and caring', as Jacobson puts it, or whether, by contrast, he thought them heartless. Parr's approach is inclusive and democratic. Foibles are endemic to the human race, and any given group or individual is capable of amusing behaviour, including himself.

Parr has repeatedly turned to the subject of his own identity throughout his career, often with comic effect. Most famously he has produced a series of assisted self-portraits, which he calls 'autoportraits'.

He has made these photographs with a variety of street and studio photographers and at photo machines, mainly at tourist sites around the world. Over time the project has grown to include Polaroids, name badges, the official portrait for his honorary degree ceremony at Manchester Metropolitan University, an online-dating profile picture and even a Chinese wedding album. Unlike other well-known photographers who have explored questions of identity through self-portraiture, such as Nikki S. Lee, Tomoko Sawada and Cindy Sherman, Parr makes no attempt to assume another identity, except insofar as the photographers' scenarios dictate. Instead, he remains himself, a global gadabout, showing up in various far-flung locations. His only affectation is his consistent deadpan expression, which undermines the prescribed formula of tourist fun.

In his autoportraits, Parr has practised judo with Vladimir Putin and floated in space like a cosmonaut. He has caught a trophy fish in Utah, drifted in a flower-strewn coracle under a flight path in Dubai and levitated in a jar of jelly beans. He has rubbed elbows with Arnold Schwarzenegger, Pierce Brosnan and Lionel Messi, and escaped from the jaws of a shark in Benidorm. He has been detained by a Nigerian soldier, taken a Turkish bride and squatted on top of the Kenyatta International Conference Centre in Nairobi. He has also appeared on a box of Wheaties cereal and served in the Georgian army. In short, he has led a life of infinite variety and epic excitement, all courtesy of the camera.

The autoportrait project celebrates a particular strain of vernacular photography, once common but increasingly usurped by mobile phone cameras and other digital technologies. Image-exchange platforms such as Snapchat enable the easy manipulation of imagery through filters, and the creation of special effects surpass even those created by professional street photographers. In spite of their eccentricities, the autoportraits represent a strand of photographic practice that will almost certainly disappear in time. Parr celebrates the imagination and inventiveness of those who make such pictures.

At the same time, the autoportraits address serious questions about photography, identity and self. In these pictures, Parr is inserted into various fictional scenarios and presented according to distinct local tastes. The portrayals themselves are often highly stylized, depending on the cultural expectations of the country where they were made. Such expectations, too, are likely to erode over time, as the exchange of photographic imagery becomes increasingly global and regional preferences are swept away. Yet none of the autoportraits, individually, serves as a credible portrait of Martin Parr; rather, they demonstrate the limitations and pitfalls of photography as a conveyor of identity.

In 1999, the Mexican photographer Graciela Iturbide connected Parr with Bruno Eslava, at that time the only remaining practitioner in Mexico City of the art of carved *fotoescultura* (photo sculptures); shrinelike statues combining photographs with wood, jewels, beads, paint and tin. Parr commissioned Eslava to produce a series of statuettes and medallions using autoportrait imagery. Typically the sculptures were used as commemorative objects, to mark the loss of a loved one. As with the autoportraits themselves, one subtext of Parr's project is the role of the vernacular photograph. Eslava was not just an accomplished craftsman; his photographic creations carried

'Ironically, as Martin Parr's fame has grown,
he has increasingly become a part of the
very same material culture he once set
out to photograph.'

extraordinary psychological charge for those who commissioned them to stand in for deceased family members – a potent mix of cherished possession and vehicle for the presence of the deceased. In co-opting this tradition, Parr also evoked his own mortality. The backgrounds removed, his face and body silhouetted against red, black and green velvet backdrops, these portraits take on a timeless, otherworldly quality.

Ironically, as Martin Parr's fame has grown, he has increasingly become a part of the very same material culture he once set out to photograph. His images have been licensed and published in countless forms, from fashion advertisements to construction siding, appearing on album covers and beer mats. Perhaps more interesting still, 'Martin Parr' has evolved subversively into a brand – the exact phenomenon he has long examined sceptically (pp. 229–233). There is now Martin Parr gin and Martin Parr beer, and M&Ms with little Martin Parr faces printed on them. There are Martin Parr puzzles and tote bags, leather jackets and sweatshirts, deck chairs and rub-on tattoos, China plates and paperweights. Martin Parr branded items became so ubiquitous for a while that fashion designer Henry Holland started a 'Martin Fucking Parr' label in 2015, simultaneously acknowledging the power of Parr's commercial identity and playfully mocking his success (p. 230, 231, 233). And when Italian artist Maurizio Cattelan and photographer Pierpaulo Ferrari invited Parr to contribute to their influential magazine *Toiletpaper*, they marked the occasion with a series of products, including a 'Shit Will Save Us' scarf (p. 233). The 'shit' in question is consumer merchandise – exactly the kind of things one can buy in the shops Parr photographs.

Photography, of course, is itself a material possession. The volume and intensity of photographic imagery that engulfs us in the twenty-first century is scarcely comprehensible. Commercial photography tells us what to do and buy, who to be and to what we should aspire. Social media tracks our activities from moment to moment. To find one's true self in the midst of all this is one of the defining challenges of our age. Fortunately, Martin Parr is there to guide us.

1   Chuck Palahniuk, *Fight Club* (New York: W.W. Norton, 1996), p. 44.

2   *Parr by Parr: Quentin Bajac Meets Martin Parr* (Amsterdam: Schilt Publishing, 2010), p. 60.

3   *Parr by Parr*, p. 81. Cartier-Bresson was responding to an exhibition of Parr's *Small World*.

4   Russell Miller, *Magnum: Fifty Years at the Frontline of History* (London: Pimlico, 1999), pp. 294–5.

5   Russell W. Belk, 'The Extended Self', *The Journal of Consumer Research*, Vol. 15, Sept. 1988, pp. 139–169.

6   Belk, p. 160.

7   Karl Marx, *Capital: A Critique of Political Economy* (1867) (New York: International Publishers, 1967), p. 71.

8   Ibid.

9   Gerry Badger, 'A Good Day Out: Reflecting on the Last Resort', in Martin Parr, *The Last Resort: Photographs of New Brighton*, revised edition (Stockport: Dewi Lewis, 2008), pp. 6–7.

10 Ibid, p. 7.

11 Colin Jacobson, 'Magnum Farce', *ZoneZero* (online publication), 1996.

19 AUG 2003 Amsterdam, NL
              18.15–19.00

Fig. 1
Hans Eijkelboom, *Photo Note*
August 19th, 2003, Amsterdam

Fig. 2
Max Yavno, *Muscle Beach,*
Los Angeles, 1949

Fig. 3
Andreas Gursky, *99 Cent*, 1999

Fig. 4
Martin Parr, four generations
out shopping together, Cribbs
Causeway Shopping Centre,
Bristol, England, 2002

Fig. 5
Lee Friedlander,
*Cray Electronics,
Chippewa Falls*, 1986

Fig. 6
Martin Parr, New Brighton,
England, from *The Last
Resort*, 1983-85

ORDINARY PORTRAITS
ONENESS
CELEBRITY

Is a picture of a person always a portrait? A collection of the photographs of 'ordinary'
people that inspired this book are joined here by two different kinds of portraits – group
portraits of club members and hobbyists taken from short films commissioned by BBC
One television on the theme of British 'oneness', and editorial portraits of the great, good
and notorious. Whether one or many, ordinary or extraordinary, the people portrayed here
are in the end, only human.

Nice, France,
2015

Norman Soper who won Best Pot Leek at the Sandwell Show,
West Bromwich, the Black Country, England, 2010

Martin Bramley, the Rhubarb Triangle, Wakefield,
West Yorkshire, England, 2015

Mark Evans with No. 21 at the Tipton Pigeon
Racing Club, the Black Country, England, 2010

Wolverhampton Races,
the Black Country, England, 2012

James Shaw, Associate MCC Member at Lord's
Cricket Ground, London, England, 2018

Yang Yi and Xi Chuang, shopping centre,
Canton Road, Hong Kong, 2013

Missionaries Matthew Tanner and Preston Toone,
Mr Mac, Salt Lake City, Utah, USA, 2015

Evelyn Marie Seidel, Lady Di Club,
Hamelin, Germany, 2013

Shelly, George and Ales Seaman, Whitby Goth
Weekend, Whitby, Yorkshire, England, 2014

Harbhajan Singh, Willenhall Market, Walsall,
the Black Country, England, 2011

Orangemen, the Twelfth, Belfast,
Northern Ireland, 2016

Crisp 'N' Fry, Spring Bank,
Hull, England, 2017

Monroe Avenue, Rochester,
New York, USA, 2012

Tim Montondo, Ward's Natural Science,
Rochester, New York, USA, 2012

Mary Lynn Myrkel, Gay Pride march,
Atlanta, Georgia, USA, 2010

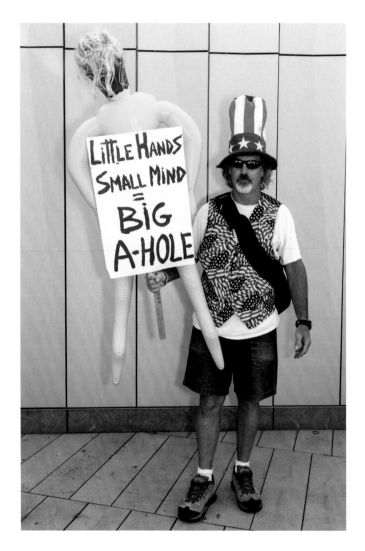

The Republican National Convention,
Cleveland, Ohio, USA, 2016

Val Yaggy, The Republican National Convention,
Cleveland, Ohio, USA, 2016

The Republican National Convention,
Cleveland, Ohio, USA, 2016

Kristen Coston, The Republican National
Convention, Cleveland, Ohio, USA, 2016

Following page: Clevedon Swimming Club,
Somerset, England, 2016

Dog walkers, Newcastle upon
Tyne, England, 2018

Junior football team, Barnet,
London, England, 2018

Lifesavers, Exmouth,
England, 2018

Allotment holders, Bearwood,
the Black Country, England, 2017

Following page: Bog snorkellers,
Llanwrtyd Wells, Wales, 2017

Central Beacons Mountain Rescue Team,
Brecon Beacons, Wales, 2016

Cavers, East Wemyss,
Scotland, 2017

Birdwatchers, Rainham Marshes,
London, England, 2017

Night kayakers, Killyleagh,
Northern Ireland, 2017

Bhangra dancers, Assembly Rooms,
Edinburgh, Scotland, 2017

Marie Clifford exercise classes,
Avonmouth, England, 2016

Roller skaters, The Coronet,
Elephant and Castle, London, England, 2017

Boxers, Birmingham,
England, 2017

Ospreys wheelchair rugby team,
Llantrisant Leisure Centre, Wales, 2016

Zandra Rhodes, designer,
London, England, 2011

Vivienne Westwood, designer,
London, England, 2012

Pelé, Brazilian footballer,
London, England, 2003

Gordon Banks, English goalkeeper who played in the 1966
World Cup victory against West Germany, England, 2003

Matt Lucas and David Walliams posing
as 'Little Britain' characters Lou and
Andy, London, England, 2006

John Shuttleworth, comedian,
Sheffield, England, 1997

Paul Smith, designer,
London, England, 2016

Zadie Smith, author,
London, England, 2010

Ai Weiwei, artist, curator and architectural
designer, Kassel, Germany, 2007

Alain de Botton, author and philosopher,
London, England, 2011

Cara Delevingne, model,
Weston-super-Mare, England, 2012

Tracey Emin, artist,
London, England, 2002

Madness, British ska band,
London, England, 1999

David Sproxton, Peter Lord and
Nick Park, founders of Aardman
Animations, Bristol, England, 2008

Paul Stephenson, activist
and civil rights campaigner,
Bristol, England, 2008

Mike Leigh, writer and director,
London, England, 1997

Hugh Collins, who served a prison sentence in HMP
Barlinnie, Glasgow, for murder. He now lives and works
in an artists' community in Cowgate, Edinburgh.
Edinburgh, Scotland, 1998

Bruce Reynolds, mastermind of the Great Train
Robbery in 1963, at the time the biggest robbery in
British history. He went on to write in the media about
cars and moral values. London, England, 1998

Anna Wintour, journalist and fashion
editor, Fashion Week, Milan, Italy, 2017

The Perry Family – daughter Florence, Philippa
and Grayson, London, England, 2012

Henry Holland, designer,
London, England, 2014

Ryan Lo, designer, London,
England, 2014

Patrick Grant, designer,
London, England, 2014

Osman Yousefzada, designer,
London, England, 2014

EVERYBODY DANCE NOW
GRAND SLAM
A DAY AT THE RACES

Sports fans and office Christmas parties; days out with the girls and having a flutter
on the horses; hen parties and pride parades and putting up with the weather; from country
dance to pole dance, and from ball to bar mitzvah: our identities are revealed as much
by how we play, celebrate and enjoy our leisure time as by our beliefs and convictions.

Hen party, Belfast,
Northern Ireland, 2008

Margate, Kent,
England, 1986

Sikh wedding, City Hall,
Cardiff, Wales, 2008

Grecians' Ball, Christ's Hospital School,
West Sussex, England, 2011

21st birthday party, Royal Nawaab,
Levenshulme, Manchester, England, 2018

The M.video Christmas party,
Moscow, Russia, 2011

Manchester Pride,
Manchester, England, 2018

Notting Hill Carnival,
London, England, 2017

Scottish Country Dance Club,
Dufftown, Scotland, 2017

Silver Swans, the Royal Academy of Dance,
London, England, 2017

Bar mitzvah, New York,
USA, 2017

Pride, Ryde, Isle of Wight,
England, 2018

Pride, Ryde, Isle of Wight,
England, 2018

Caledonian Ball, London,
England, 2013

Dinner dance, The Savoy,
London, England, 2016

Dunston Social Club, Newcastle
upon Tyne, England, 2008

Sexy Sunday, Whitby Goth Weekend,
Spa Pavilion, Whitby, Yorkshire, England, 2014

New Model Army,
Whitby Goth Weekend,
Spa Pavilion, Whitby,
Yorkshire, England, 2014

Magdalene Ball, Cambridge,
England, 2015

Australian Open, Melbourne,
Australia, 2018

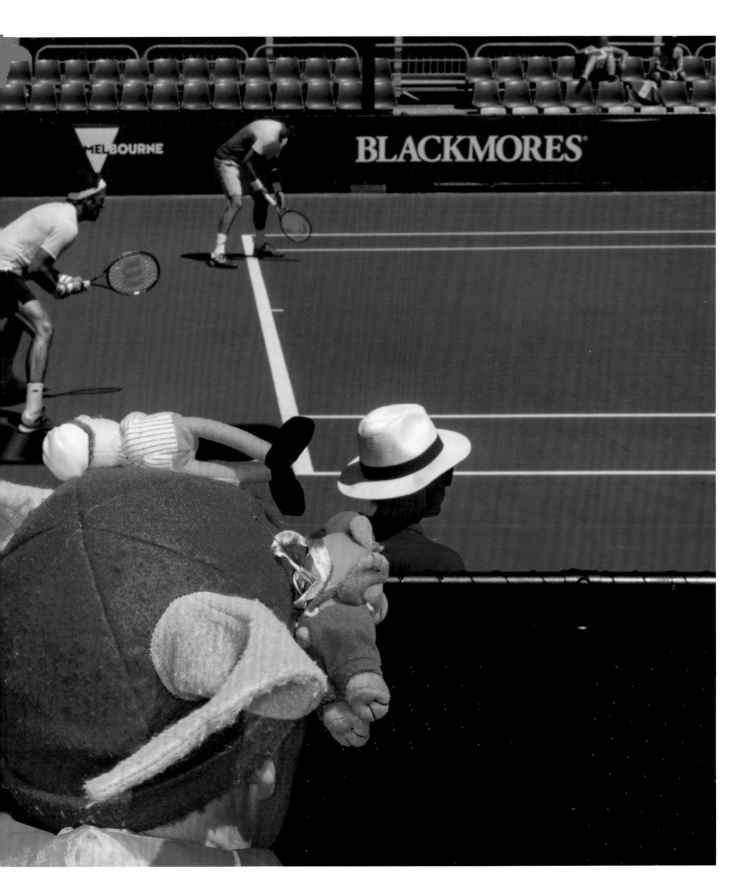

French Open, Paris,
France, 2016

French Open, Paris,
France, 2016

US Open, New York,
USA, 2016

US Open, New York,
USA, 2017

The Championships,
Wimbledon, England, 2015

US Open, New York,
USA, 2017

The Championships, Wimbledon,
England, 2015

Australian Open, Melbourne,
Australia, 2018

French Open, Paris,
France, 2016

Australian Open, Melbourne,
Australia, 2018

Australian Open, Melbourne,
Australia, 2018

Rafael Nadal, US Open,
New York, USA, 2017

Kentucky Derby, Louisville,
USA, 2015

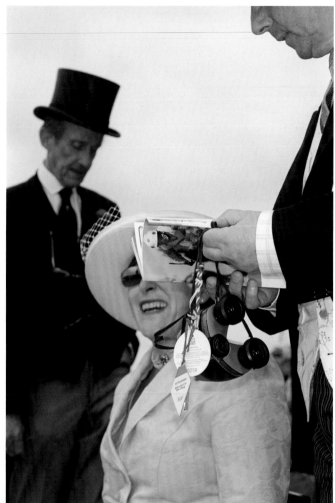

The Derby, Epsom, Surrey,
England, 2004

The Derby, Epsom, Surrey,
England, 2004

The Derby, Epsom, Surrey,
England, 2004

Royal Ascot, Berkshire,
England, 1999

Royal Ascot, Berkshire,
England, 2013

Melbourne Cup,
Australia, 2008

Dubai World Cup, United
Arab Emirates, 2007

The Cheltenham Gold Cup,
Gloucestershire, England, 2006

The Grand National, Aintree,
Merseyside, England, 2018

Ladies Day, The Grand National,
Aintree, Merseyside, England, 2016

Ladies Day, The Grand National,
Aintree, Merseyside, England, 2016

The Grand National, Aintree,
Merseyside, England, 2018

Durban July races, Durban,
South Africa, 2005

The Grand National, Aintree,
Merseyside, England, 2018

THE
BRITISH
QUESTION

Sir Benjamin Stone knew a thing or two about politics. So when the Edwardian photographer and Conservative MP launched a groundbreaking new photography initiative in the summer of 1897, he hosted a special event at one of London's most luxurious hotels, Sir George Gilbert Scott's Midland Grand, the centrepiece of St Pancras railway station. Assured of a healthy attendance, Stone proceeded to invite a veritable 'who's who' of representatives from learned British institutions. The Royal Society, the Society of Antiquaries, the Royal Institute of British Architects, the newly created National Trust and the Royal Geographic Society all sent delegates, as did several prominent photo clubs, including the Royal Photographic Society, the Amateur Photographic Association and the photographic societies of Birmingham and Liverpool.[1] Also present were Charles Darwin's son Leonard (then a sitting MP from the Liberal opposition in Parliament), two trustees of the British Museum, and the head of the Science and Art Department of the South Kensington Museum, the influential scientist and photographer Captain William de Wiveleslie Abney.[2] 'It must be obvious to everyone nowadays,' Stone explained to the assembled experts, 'that current history is being largely recorded in photographic pictures.'[3] The trouble, Stone went on, was that whilst interesting pictures were being made all the time, they were spontaneous and unplanned, and consequently of little use to historians and other analysts. A system was needed. It was 'almost a national duty,' he affirmed, 'that photographic records of our time be collected and preserved for the use and instruction of those who are to follow us.'[4]

Although not engaged in a formal survey himself, Martin Parr, more than any other photographer, has taken up Stone's gauntlet of recording the people, places and things that make Britain distinctive. Over the thirteen years that it was active, Stone's National Photographic Record Association, or NPRA as it would become known, contributed 5,883 prints to an archive at the British Museum, of which Stone himself gave slightly more than a quarter: 1,532.[5] By comparison, at the time of writing, Parr has added more than 47,000 photographs to the Magnum Photos website, of which nearly 21,000 are pictures of Britain.[6] These range from his very first photographs, made in the late 1960s and early 1970s, to the present day. Britain, and more particularly, the lives, habits and peculiarities of ordinary Britons, is the subject with which Parr is most often identified, and the subject he has revisited consistently throughout his career. It has also been the inspiration for numerous books, including some of his best known: *The Last Resort* (1986), *The Cost of Living* (1989), *Signs of the Times* (1992), *Think of England* (2000), *Black Country Stories* (2014), *The Rhubarb Triangle* (2016), *Remote Scottish Postboxes* (2017) and *Think of Scotland* (2017), to name only the most conspicuous examples.

Parr's interest in British life dates to his earliest days as a photographer. As a secondary-school student aged fifteen in 1967, he produced his first photo essay on Harry Ramsden's fish and chip shop in Guiseley on the outskirts of Leeds. (Prior to its chain expansion during the 1980s, the original Harry Ramsden's restaurant was said to be the largest chippy in the world.) The two black-and-white photographs preserved from this series foreshadow what would become Parr's signature style (fig. 1). In one, a family crowd around a table at the far end of the restaurant eating their dinner, the rest of the tables unoccupied, a red phone box in the distance. The picture is taken

'Over the course of Parr's career, no subject has occupied him more comprehensively, or more consistently, than the countless small things that make Britain what it is. He probes the clichés of British life – cups of tea and English breakfasts, rhubarb, umbrellas and sticks of rock – giving them fresh consideration.'

from an acute angle, making the family look tiny and distant at the end of the row whilst the tables and seats in the foreground are pushed this way and that, the table surfaces dotted with salt shakers and bottles of vinegar. The diners occupy only about a third of the frame, indifferent to the disorder around them and almost existentially occupied with their meal.

In the other photograph, a well-dressed man and woman sit between two tables holding hands, the salt and vinegar this time perfectly framed by the cross bars of a privacy screen, with the rectangular shapes of the screen, tables and chairs playing against the brick wall behind. Though positioned in the centre of the composition, the people nevertheless seem incidental, enshrined in the melancholy interior. In each photograph, the harsh direct light of overhead fluorescent bulbs adds to the unsettling mood.

Parr frequently photographs in series. Some of these series are long and open-ended, as with his photographs of people dancing around the world (pp. 88–107). Dance, for Parr, is a great leveller, whether it is a group of young women in Newcastle wearing plastic fire hats and playing at pole dancing, pensioners practising moves by the Margate Lido, middle-aged skinheads tangling in the mosh pit at a New Model Army concert or a Sikh family celebrating a wedding at Cardiff's City Hall (pp. 89, 90–91, 104–105, 92). Utterly joyous, these pictures show people pursuing personal tastes and interests, innocent in their enthusiasm and gathering with like-minded others. For Parr, these pictures have their origins in a touching series he made as a student in 1970 of ballroom dancers in Blackpool, as well as dances and music therapy sessions he photographed at the Prestwich Mental Hospital in 1972 and dancing in

pubs and meeting halls in Moss Side and Longsight, inner-city Manchester, in 1972–3.

Over the course of Parr's career, no subject has occupied him more comprehensively, or more consistently, than the countless small things that make Britain what it is. He probes the clichés of British life – cups of tea and English breakfasts, rhubarb, umbrellas and sticks of rock – giving them fresh consideration: a young rugby player in his bespoke finery at Harrow, then again covered in mud after winning a match (pp. 200–201); rain at Wimbledon, showy hats at Ascot and luxuriant blooms at the Chelsea Flower Show (pp. 114, 124, 169); a queue forming at an ice-cream van on the sands at Tenby; or swimmers lining up for a punishing 'Winter Dip' in Bristol (pp. 180–181). At the same time, he photographs aspects of life in Britain that do not quite fit the stereotypes. Quiet, unheralded moments, as when a girl in a black blouse and mini-skirt makes eye contact as she looks back over her shoulder, absently chewing her nails (p. 173). Or the riotous interior of a limousine on a hen night, complete with naughty novelty blow-up doll (p. 172). Or three older women sitting silently in a row at a hairdresser in West Bromwich, sipping drinks whilst their hair is set in curlers under hood-dryers, the stuccoed wall behind them hung with family pictures and posters of models (p. 175). Such closely observational portrayals of British life form partial narratives of a kind nearly all Britons intuitively know and recognize, even if they have not experienced them first-hand.

As his fame grew in the late 1980s and 1990s, Parr began increasingly to travel on assignment, incorporating imagery made in other countries more fully into his work. His interest in global tourism and what might be described as 'Americanization' (although the term has perhaps outlived its usefulness, since British and many other foreign entities now go toe-to-toe with American companies in name-brand consumerism) resulted in the book *Small World* (1995), a playful examination of travel culture, especially at popular tourist hotspots. For the following book, *Common Sense* (1999), the theme shifted to more general concerns about consumerism, told in closely observed vignettes photographed so tightly that geography is all but erased. This period of relative de-immersion from British culture allowed Parr to return to British subjects anew with *Think of England* in 2000.

Something similar had happened at least once before in his career. Having developed a remarkable body of black-and-white work in the mid-1970s whilst living in Hebden Bridge, West Yorkshire, the artist and his wife Susie moved to County Roscommon in Ireland, where they lived from 1980 to 1983. On returning to England they settled in Merseyside, where Martin reset his approach, photographing seriously in colour and using flash for outdoor scenes. It was during this period that he produced the landmark series *The Last Resort*.

Parr's international travel has also enabled him to examine the phenomenon of 'Britishness' in other countries, especially former colonies. He has collected these in a series he calls 'British Abroad', examining vestiges of British expatriate communities and customs, particularly in India, Sri Lanka, Kenya, South Africa and Zimbabwe. Whether golfing at the Royal Harare Golf Club, playing lawn bowls at the Karen Country Club in Nairobi, picnicking on the lawn at Borrowdale Racecourse in Zimbabwe, or sipping tea in Nuwara Eliya, Sri Lanka (pp. 202–214), Parr shows post-colonial societies in which white privilege persists, despite political and economic reforms. At the same time, he reveals communities out of step with contemporary British mores, clinging to habits and fashions long since outgrown back home. These communities maintain a fantasy version of Britain that probably never existed in the UK itself, but which is now preserved, like an insect trapped in amber, in small pockets around the world.

Since the turn of the millennium, Parr has embarked on several new projects relating to the subject of British national character. In 2009, he was commissioned to photograph behind the scenes at King's College, Cambridge, for what would become *A Book of King's* (2012); it was the first in a series Parr would come to think of as 'The Establishment'. King's was followed by a series of photographs made at Harrow School (2010), Christ's Hospital School, West Sussex (2010), the City of London (2013), the British Army in Germany (2013–4), Oxford University (2014–6) and the Magdalene College Ball at Cambridge (2015). Photographs from each of these series are included in this volume (pp. 184–201). And, although not overtly critical, Parr's 'Establishment' photographs are among his most political. 'Elite groups still run the country,' Parr has explained. In the City of London in particular, 'It's still white and middle class: you rarely see anyone of colour in a livery company, [or] women. This is more to do with how the country is run and how secret and feudal it is.'[7]

The members of Parr's establishment are bound together through a series of arcane rituals, the ostensible purpose of which has long since become

'Brexit is not only one of the biggest socio-political events of our time, comparable to the rise of populism and nationalism in countries from the United States to Italy, it is also a curious manifestation of British identity.'

immaterial: toasting the Queen after the annual Swan Upping, in which mute swans on the Thames are rounded up and banded by members of the Vintners and Dyers' livery companies to assert their ownership of the birds, which they share with the crown (p. 198); Oxford University bedels (honorary officials) holding gold maces diagonally across their bodies as they prepare for a ceremony (p. 198); or Chris Patten, Hong Kong's last colonial governor and current Chancellor of Oxford University, crossing a plaza with a page boy hired to attend to him holding his flowing gown off the ground (p. 197).

In 2016, after the Brexit referendum vote to leave the European Union, Parr started a new project, photographing industries that enjoyed protected domain status under European rules, but which appeared likely to lose those protections after Brexit. Among these were Stilton cheese from Melton Mowbray, Rutland ale, Whitstable oysters, Gloucester Old Spot pork and Grimsby smoked fish. In Parr's photograph of Grimsby fishermen (p. 157), four men proudly hold filleting knives to their chests, their hands stained with fish blood. Like Brexit itself, it is a grisly business – are their knives held in defence, or in an ironic gesture of economic *hara-kiri*?

For someone like Parr who has spent much of his career exploring British identity, Brexit is not only one of the biggest socio-political events of our time, comparable to the rise of populism and nationalism in countries from the United States to Italy, it is also a curious manifestation of British identity. Voters decided to leave or remain based on a variety of factors, including their perception of economic interests and understanding of the European Union's efficacy, responsiveness and ability to solve problems that matter, as well as the voters' views on the future potential of a unified Europe as a vehicle for growth and maintaining peace. Politicians on both sides of the debate also used the occasion of the referendum to discuss immigration and its impact on 'traditional' British society and culture. At its most extreme, this degenerated into a nationalistic argument for the status quo, or indeed, for rewinding the clock to a time when widespread immigration had not affected communities across Britain. By this logic, a vote to leave Europe was fundamentally about resisting change, rejecting the European way of doing things and returning to a more purely 'British' culture, however that might be defined. In response, Parr travelled to those areas where separatist sentiment was strongest.

The Brexit debate parallels the rise of nationalist movements in the United States, Hungary, Poland and Italy, and the revival of far-right factions in Austria, Germany and France. Yet Parr provides little evidence of the uglier side of British separatism, or indeed, of simmering Scottish and Welsh nationalist sentiments or ongoing tensions in Northern Ireland. Parr shows us that politics is an abstract affair to most citizens, particularly beyond the M25 where central government actions can feel especially remote. The people in Parr's photographs are simply getting on with things, expressing their patriotism perhaps, but participating in fetes and festivals much as they always have done, queuing, shopping and meeting up for a drink. Indeed it is remarkable how normal everything seems, even though economic disparities are apparent. Since pollsters tell us that pensioners supported Brexit more than almost any other demographic, Parr also shows older sitters repeatedly, their lonely and withdrawn figures perhaps a metaphor for Brexit sympathies.

**'Does it even make sense to speak of Britain
or the British people, let alone attempt to
describe them visually?'**

In Parr's Brexit Britain, an old woman walks her dog obliviously past a Sainsbury's shop window with a giant photograph of a croissant, the consummate European emblem, towering behind her (p. 174). A chained pit bull terrier in an England jersey sits sleepily as two women watch a St George's Day parade in the background, covered almost head to toe in patriotic finery, one even wearing a red-and-white plastic lei (p. 149). Children stare intensely from behind England face paint, their heads crowned with flags and Cross of St George antennae (p. 150). A group of girls gather on the Ulster Protestant celebration of the Twelfth of July, whilst a family eats ice creams at the Royal Welsh Show in Builth Wells (pp. 173, 168). It is, potentially, the calm before the storm – the red warning flag on a Cornish beach is the only hint of possible trouble to come (pp. 182–183).

In contrast to Benjamin Stone and his NPRA, which sought to create a logical and ordered survey, Parr gravitates towards the spontaneous and unexpected. Although he plans his travels carefully around specific events and situations, he rarely poses his subjects, preferring instead to capture activity as it unfolds. The Britain Parr reveals is prone to absurdity and quirky humour. It is a place where eccentricity is a birthright and pretension is gleefully deflated. Parr's is the England of Spike Milligan's famous ode to National Health Service dentistry:

English Teeth, English Teeth!
Shining in the sun
A part of British heritage
Aye, each and every one.
English Teeth, Happy Teeth!
Always having fun
Clamping down on bits of fish
And sausages half done.

English Teeth! HEROES' Teeth!
Hear them click! and clack!
Let's sing a song of praise to them –
Three Cheers for the Brown Grey and Black.[8]

Despite its dark humour, Milligan's poem, like Parr's photographs, contains a message of encouragement. Never mind that you're imperfect: we're all imperfect! The weather is awful, and we eat food at times that would make a gourmet weep. In fact, our situation may be ludicrous – but we're all in it together and we can laugh about it. Where else on earth would grey-haired men camp out in jackets and ties for tickets to a cricket match (p. 161)? Or a prized fuschia so thoroughly take over a woman's wheelchair that plant and owner seem to have become one (p. 169)? Or a man turn out on his horse for a fox hunt in full regalia, next to a parking sign that reads, 'Have you paid and displayed a valid ticket?' (p. 177). Being British means carrying on undeterred, despite these foibles.

Besides, appearances can be deceiving. Consider pigeon breeder Mark Evans, whose big, beefy hands, dry and nicked from labour, delicately cradle a pigeon at the Racing Club in Tipton (p. 43). Parr made a short film following Evans to Mongolia, where he went to recover a group of racing birds. Evans's reflections on the birds, their travels and the implications of industrial development in Central Asia provide an unexpectedly poignant turn in a distinctly British story.

To photograph something as nebulous, dynamic and diverse as Britain poses seemingly insurmountable challenges. Britain is not a place so much as it is an infinite array of experiences, some shared and some private. Not only does the would-be photographer

'This is another stereotypically British trait:
the belief that there should *always* be
walnut whips and sherbet dabs, "Eastenders"
and "The Archers".'

of British life have to consider the autonomous identities of Northern Island, Scotland, England, Wales, the Channel Islands and the Isle of Man, but also the regional characteristics that separate Geordie from Glaswegian, and Brummie from Scouse. Even within these communities there are divisions based on neighbourhood, wealth, occupation and political, religious and ethnic affiliation. There are distinctions between urban and rural, young and old, and male, female and LGBTQ communities. Among these, there are also self-selecting communities: speed-metal bikers and folk dance revivalists, canal enthusiasts and technopunks. Do such people really have anything in common? Does it even make sense to speak of Britain or the British people, let alone attempt to describe them visually?

Over the course of the medium's history, many photographers have tried to portray the salient ingredients of British life. Some, like Benjamin Stone, favoured a formal approach. Indeed, one might reasonably argue that a photographic survey is a distinctly British undertaking. Although other countries have had surveys – the German photographer August Sander's *People of the Twentieth Century* is possibly the best-known example – in Britain there have been a disproportionate number, beginning with Alexander Agassiz's failed attempt in the 1860s to create a photographic record of the various diverse peoples of the British Empire. A half-century later, the National Portrait Gallery collaborated with photographer Walter Stoneman to create the National Photographic Record (not to be confused with Benjamin Stone's NPRA), a photographic encyclopaedia of people whom he and his advisors held to be key figures in British society. Whilst Sander attempted to find German archetypes

– people who somehow embodied an occupation or social position, such as 'a cook' or 'a bricklayer' – Stoneman aimed to find actual persons of influence, in order to record the people who were making history, even as it was being written. His plan was to depict each subject in a single photographic portrait produced according to a rigorous protocol: head and shoulders, looking towards the camera, against a dark neutral background. Begun in 1917, the scheme had a remarkably long run, ending only in 1970, twelve years after Stoneman's death.

Benjamin Stone's answer to the 'Britain' puzzle was to carve up the map geographically, identifying rituals, ceremonies and traditions he believed were in danger of disappearing, and methodically recording them. He and his associates focused primarily on village and rural life, which Stone believed to be most under threat. Justified as a matter of historical and anthropological interest, the project was nonetheless infused with nostalgia and a small 'c' conservative desire that the quaint things in life not change, even if we do not participate in them ourselves. This, paradoxically, is another stereotypically British trait: the belief that there should *always* be walnut whips and sherbet dabs, 'Eastenders' and 'The Archers', that these things are somehow hard-wired to the British experience. As the Kinks proclaimed in 1968:

We are the Village Green Preservation Society ...
God save strawberry jam and all the different varieties.[9]

Britishness may be complex and difficult to define, and its ingredients constantly in flux, yet there will always be those determined to preserve it.

'Although "oneness" in Britain does not yet
extend to full racial equality, Parr shows us
a country that is growing in cultural
and ethnic diversity.'

Stone's photograph of participants in the annual Abbots Bromley Horn Dance shows a side of Britain few would have recognized in the waning days of empire (fig. 2). Even as it rose to superpower status, Stone discovered, Britain had retained many obscure traditions. The Horn Dance, still performed, is unique to the village of Abbots Bromley in Staffordshire, not far from Stone's parliamentary seat in Birmingham. The dance consists of twelve performers, all from the same family, although Stone only captured eleven in his photograph. The last, a male 'Maid Marion' dressed in lady's clothing, evidently preferred the photographer not to record him for posterity. Six dancers wearing patterned trousers hold reindeer horns shoulder high, whilst one boy holds a bow, another a bell and a young dancer grips a hobbyhorse.[10] A jester, the star of the picture, stands just off centre, his floppy pointed hat leaning sideways, with little round bells crossing his forehead like an off-kilter fringe, as he addresses the camera squarely. His fellow dancers also face forward, showing off their equipment seemingly without affect, as if their surreal performance were utterly unremarkable. Stone may have set out to make emotionally detached, inscrutable documents, but that is not the reason his images succeed. Rather, it is the things Stone could not control – the subtleties of gesture and expression, the cracks that emerge from beneath the thin veneer of order, that makes them so compelling.

If Parr's photographs of bog snorkellers in Llanwrtyd Wells or dog walkers in Newcastle (pp. 60–61, 58) call to mind Stone's horn dancers, it is precisely because the subjects display this same irrepressible quality. The bog snorkelling photograph was originally commissioned by BBC One television in 2016, as part of a series of 30-second films on the subject

of British 'oneness'. Each session also included the creation of a still photograph (pp. 56–67). Parr chose to show groups of volunteers and hobbyists engaged in shared interests in diverse communities across Britain – night kayakers in Northern Ireland, for example, mountain rescuers in the Brecon Beacons, cavers in County Fife, wheelchair rugby players in Glamorgan, Bhangra dancers in Edinburgh and roller skaters in south London. The resulting films were then used as television 'idents' – short spacers between programmes to identify the broadcaster. In each of the films, the subjects pause momentarily, to face and acknowledge the camera, but otherwise chat amongst themselves, performing the activity they enjoy unselfconsciously.

Although 'oneness' in Britain does not yet extend to full racial equality, Parr shows us a country that is growing in cultural and ethnic diversity. A parade group proudly holds up a model of the *Empire Windrush*, the passenger ship that famously brought more than a thousand West Indian voyagers to Britain in 1948, many of whom would settle in the country (p. 164). The model is powerful in light of the Windrush scandal, too, in which Windrush-generation immigrants were controversially detained or deported under Home Secretary Amber Rudd, forcing her resignation in April 2018. Separately, a jubilant crowd packs a city street in Bristol, ending their Ramadan fast at Iftar (pp. 162–163). In Clacton, a group of Hindu women celebrate the end of the Shravan month by making a representation of Lord Shiva in the sand, dipping their feet in the sea and laying out candles and food as offerings, with the turbines of a wind farm in the distance (pp. 216–217). And at the Notting Hill Carnival, a group of young women, resplendent in their elaborate coloured costumes, sit on the kerb tucking into takeaway lunches, as one adjusts her makeup using her mobile phone as a mirror (pp. 166–167).

It now seems ironic that Stone chose the Midland Grand Hotel to launch an initiative intended to preserve British cultural identity. More than a century later, the rebranded St Pancras Renaissance is the terminus for Eurostar trains between London and Paris, Brussels and Amsterdam, depositing thousands of visitors into the centre of the city every day. The Channel Tunnel has long been a lightning rod for those who believe the infusion of visitors it encourages dilutes British national character. Even in Stone's day, the digging of a cross-channel tunnel was considered highly controversial, and a pilot project started in Dover was shut down, ostensibly on grounds of national defence. By coincidence, in 2003, Parr created an advertising campaign for the Eurostar company, mainly featuring 'typically British' objects photographed from above to resemble Eurostar's circular logo, including a polo mint on a tongue, a Jammie Dodger, a cup of tea and a moulded green jelly on a plate.

For someone who has assumed the role of ambassador for photography internationally, Parr has long been a champion of British photographers, especially of those similarly engaged in social documentary practice. Benjamin Stone may have been the first photographer to attempt to create a comprehensive photographic document of the British, but he was far from the last. Parr understands this history well, and has frequently acknowledged the influence of other practitioners on his work. He has long professed his admiration for like-minded contemporaries, including David Hurn, Chris Killip, Markéta

Luskačová and Tom Wood. Widely recognized as an authority on photographic history, he has published three volumes of the landmark *The Photobook: A History* with collaborator Gerry Badger (2004, 2009 and 2014) and has also edited *The Chinese Photobook*, with Wassink Lundgren (2016). Recently, as he has become more active as a curator, Parr has also begun to reveal the broader scope of his appreciation for other contemporary photographers and their predecessors, as with *Strange and Familiar: Britain as Revealed by International Photographers* at London's Barbican and the Manchester Art Gallery (2016) and *The Great British Seaside: Photography from the 1960s to the Present* at the National Maritime Museum in Greenwich (2017). The launch of the Martin Parr Foundation in 2017 reflects another element of this vision – it has rapidly acquired key archives relating to the practice of social documentary photography in the United Kingdom and Ireland.

Much has been written about Parr's interest in the English photographer Tony Ray-Jones, whose life was abruptly cut short at the age of thirty-one. Ray-Jones's influence on Parr was the subject of the exhibition and catalogue *Only in England: Photographs by Tony Ray-Jones and Martin Parr* at the Science Museum, London, in 2013. Intriguingly, Stone's influence on Tony-Ray Jones is well documented, since he owned a volume of Stone's pictures that he found in a junk shop.[11] A precocious talent, Ray-Jones began his studies at the London College of Printing, earning a scholarship to the Yale University School of Art in 1960. In nearby New York, he met the legendary art director for *Harper's Bazaar,* Alexey Brodovitch, who counted Robert Frank, Irving Penn and Garry Winogrand among his students. Ray-Jones studied with

Brodovitch between 1962–3; they had met in Richard Avedon's studio.

Ray-Jones graduated from Yale in 1964 and returned to England in 1966, buying a camper van in which he travelled the length and breadth of Britain, taking photographs. Inspired in part by Stone, he recorded British habits and eccentricities, focusing on seaside holidays, sporting events, beauty pageants and family outings. He hoped to publish these in a book, but did not survive to see the project completed; after a brief stint teaching in San Francisco, he contracted leukaemia and died in 1972, just as Parr was completing his studies in England. The maquette for Ray-Jones's planned book was completed posthumously and published in 1974 as *A Day Off: An English Journal*. Along with the travelling exhibition that preceded it, it would have a profound effect on photographers throughout the country, including Parr. Mischievous without being unkind, and full of humour and insight, it remains one of the landmark works of British photography.

Ray-Jones was restlessly inventive, but he did not create the genre himself; he, in turn, was indebted to countless famous and lesser-known photographers who had worked for pictorial magazines in the postwar period. In Britain, the two dominant publications were the light-hearted and largely apolitical *Lilliput* and the more handsomely illustrated, news-orientated *Picture Post*. Both published photographs on 'human interest' subjects, often tinged with humour, such as Bert Hardy's photograph of two teenagers dancing in a Rochdale music hall, published in *Picture Post* in 1957 (fig. 3). In what looks like a lost image from Parr's own dance series, Hardy shows a boy and girl dancing with abandon inside a hall briefly illuminated by flash, the light particularly harsh on the girl, who is closest to the camera, with deep shadow falling away rapidly. The girl shifts her arms and feet awkwardly, passing one arm over her head and holding the other across her waist. Meanwhile, the boy's trousers flap and cling to his legs inelegantly, his left trouser leg riding up his sock, the floor scuffed and dirty. It is a picture of two people being discovered by a photographer when they least expected it, their inhibitions cast to the wind. They may look clumsy to an outsider but, like Spike Milligan's teeth, who is there to criticize them?

Bill Brandt was another of the photographers who appeared in the pages of *Picture Post, Lilliput* and other pictorial magazines of the 1930s and 1940s whose work would later influence Parr and others. The German-born Brandt arrived in England in 1931, having served as Man Ray's apprentice in Paris for several months in 1930. In 1936, Brandt published the most direct precursor to Ray-Jones's *A Day Off*, a book of sixty-three photographs of English life entitled *The English at Home*. The original idea for the book was to juxtapose scenes of wealth and privilege – many of which were of Brandt's extended family – with pictures of people living in poverty, arranged on facing pages. A more nuanced arrangement prevailed in the published version, in which photographs were arranged according to a narrative progression and visual impact, rather than any set formula. Several pictures in the book grew to become some of Brandt's most celebrated works, including *Kensington Children's Party* (fig. 4). In the picture, helium balloons look like balls on the ends of sticks, held impossibly stiff and upright by their ribbons. A bright flash casts black shadows across the curtains. Two children in the lower right seem like out-of-focus apparitions,

'It is not satirical, in the sense of seeking to make fun of another's weakness, so much as it is knowing and appreciative of the idiosyncrasies of British national character.'

whilst a girl in the background behind them looks at the camera with one eye, half of her face and body cut off by the frame. Near the centre stands a boy, arms at his side, staring transfixed at the camera. In the background behind him is a girl wearing a floral garland – the birthday girl, perhaps? – her lips smeared with dark lipstick. The overall effect is of somewhere strange and artificial, a timeless product of the imagination rather than the camera.

If Parr's photographs display some of this same surreal quality, it is testament to the rich lineage of photographic practice in Britain. And it is also because in Britain, real and artificial are sometimes difficult to distinguish, and intention does not always meet reality. Such irreconcilable contradictions have given rise to a particular brand of absurdist comedy, admired throughout the world. When John Cleese performed his 'Silly Walk' in 'Monty Python's Flying Circus', the humour lay not just in his exaggerated gait in a bowler hat and three-piece suit but in his earnest attempt to please his employers, the Ministry of Silly Walks, by inventing a stride like no other (fig. 5). He did not set the rules, he only attempted to abide by them. Parr's photography is heir to this rich comedic tradition, recognizable in David Walliams' and Matt Lucas's 'Little Britain' characters of Lou and Andy (p. 72) and expressed whenever John Shuttleworth feels the need to check the level of the local reservoir (p. 73). It is not satirical, in that it seeks to make fun of another's weakness, so much as it is knowing and appreciative of the idiosyncrasies of British national character.

Britain, after all, is a set of attitudes and a state of mind – as Parr shows us, it is not a fixed identity. Nor is it simply an association of neighbouring nations or a stale bread baked only of Celts, Picts, Angles, Saxons and other northern European tribes. It is not even a particular place or a meteorological condition, although both inevitably play into its character. It is a peculiar seam in humanity, truly international in scope, born in equal measure of breathtaking achievement and glaring weakness, unspeakable selfishness and touching compassion, freedom and restraint, hubris and humility. It is not an ideal or a standard, or about adherence to certain rules (although rules are most welcome here). It is welcoming and repulsive, frustrating and beguiling. One laughs at it, even as it laughs at itself. It is just as Martin Parr has photographed it.

1   'Notes of the Month', *The Antiquary*, August 1897, vol. xxxiii, p. 226.
2   'The National Photographic Association', *Photography*, 15 July 1897, no. 453, vol. ix, p. 438.
3   Ibid.
4   Ibid.
5   Elizabeth Edwards and Peter James, *A Record of England: Sir Benjamin Stone & The National Photographic Record Association 1897–1910* (Stockport: Dewi Lewis, 2006), p. 23. In 2000, the British Museum transferred the collection to the V&A.
6   magnumphotos.com, September 2018. Not counted in the 'Britain' figure are pictures from Ireland, which Stone would have included as a British nation.
7   Martin Parr quoted by Hettie Judah, in 'Photographer Martin Parr on being back in vogue – and setting his sights on the British establishment', *Independent*, 8 February 2016.
8   Spike Milligan, 'Teeth', first published in *Silly Verse for Kids* (London: Dennis Dobson, 1959).
9   The Kinks, 'The Kinks are the Village Green Preservation Society', 1968.
10 With apologies to Ernst Gombrich: 'Indeed it abhors frills...' *Meditations on a Hobby Horse and other Essays on the Theory of Art* (London and New York: Phaidon, 1978).
11 Russell Roberts, Tony Ray-Jones (London: Chris Boot, 2004), p. 17.

'To photograph something as nebulous, dynamic and diverse as Britain poses seemingly insurmountable challenges. Britain is not a place so much as it is an infinite array of experiences, some shared and some private. Not only does the would-be photographer of British life have to consider the autonomous identities of Northern Island, Scotland, England, Wales, the Channel Islands and the Isle of Man, but also the regional characteristics that separate Geordie from Glaswegian, and Brummie from Scouse.'

Fig. 1
Martin's first photo essay about
Harry Ramsden's fish and chip shop,
England, 1967

Fig. 3
Bert Hardy, two teenagers at a dance hall in
Rochdale, Lancashire, from the series 'The
Truth About Teenagers', 1957

Fig. 2
Sir John Benjamin Stone, *The Players in
the Abbots Bromley Horn Dance*, c.1900

Fig. 4
Bill Brandt, *Kensington Children's
Party*, c.1934

Fig. 5
The Ministry of Silly Walks from
'Monty Python's Flying Circus', 1970

BRITAIN AT THE TIME OF BREXIT
THE ESTABLISHMENT

A portrait of Britain at a time of both change and retrospection, when tradition and the 'Great British Identity' are being questioned, championed and renounced. In the years leading up to and after the 2016 Brexit referendum on membership in the European Union, Martin Parr documented the spirit of modern Britain, particularly in areas with high concentrations of 'Leave' voters. At the same time, he has continued to explore some of the bastions of the British establishment – the City of London, Cambridge, Oxford, Harrow and Christ's Hospital School.

Stone Cross Parade, St George's Day,
West Bromwich, the Black Country, England, 2017

Stone Cross Parade, St George's Day,
West Bromwich, the Black Country, England, 2017

British citizenship ceremony,
Bristol Registry Office, Bristol, England, 2017

The Bon Accord Shopping Centre,
Aberdeen, Scotland, 2017

Stack It High, Hessle Road,
Hull, England, 2017

Preparing lobster pots, Newlyn Harbour,
Cornwall, England, 2018

Brian and Ross Cartwright, Griffin-Woodhouse Ltd
chain makers, Cradley Heath, Sandwell,
the Black Country, England, 2010

Traditional smoked haddock, Alfred Enderby Ltd,
Grimsby, England, 2016

Stone Cross Parade, St George's Day, West Bromwich,
the Black Country, England, 2017

Stone Cross Parade, St George's Day, West Bromwich,
the Black Country, England, 2017

Street party for the royal wedding of Prince Harry
and Meghan Markle, Stockport, England, 2018

Stone Cross Parade, St George's Day, West
Bromwich, the Black Country, England, 2017

Lord's Cricket Ground, London,
England, 2018

Lord's Cricket Ground, London,
England, 2018

Iftar festival, St Mark's Road,
Bristol, England, 2018

Windrush boat, St Paul's Carnival,
Bristol, England, 2018

St Paul's Carnival, Bristol,
England, 2018

Notting Hill Carnival,
London, England, 2017

Methodist Church summer fete,
Mousehole, Cornwall, England, 2017

Royal Welsh Show,
Builth Wells, Wales, 2018

Saturday sell-off, RHS Chelsea
Flower Show, London, England, 2018

RHS Chelsea Flower Show,
London, England, 2018

Party for the royal wedding of
Prince Harry and Meghan Markle,
Didsbury, Manchester, England, 2018

Car boot sale, Bristol,
England, 2016

Hen party, Hollywood Cars,
Aberdeen, Scotland, 2017

North Somerset Young Farmers Barn Dance,   The Twelfth, Belfast,
Langford, Somerset, England, 2017   Northern Ireland, 2018

Sainsbury's, Chanterlands Avenue,
Hull, England, 2017

Susan's hairdressers, West Bromwich,
the Black Country, England, 2011

Henley Royal Regatta,
Henley-on-Thames, England, 2016

South Wold Hunt, Louth,
Lincolnshire, England, 2015

Lincolnshire Show, Lincolnshire,
England, 2018

Lincolnshire Show, Lincolnshire,
England, 2018

Henleaze Lake, Bristol,
England, 2018

Henleaze Lake, Bristol,
England, 2018

Following page: Porthcurno,
Cornwall, England, 2017

Christ's Hospital School,
West Sussex, England, 2010

The Duke of Beaufort's Boxing Day Hunt,
Cirencester Park, Gloucestershire, England, 2016

The Queen visiting the Livery Hall of the Drapers'
Livery Company for their 650th anniversary,
the City of London, London, England, 2014

Christ's Hospital School,
West Sussex, England, 2010

Harrow School, London,
England, 2011

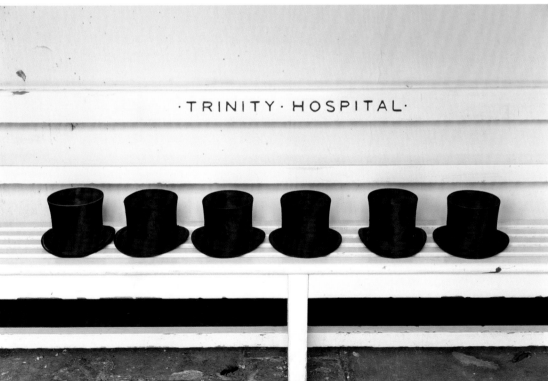

The Silent Ceremony to swear in the new Lord Mayor,
Fiona Woolf, Guildhall, the City of London,
London, England, 2013

The Mercers' Company at
Trinity Hospital in Greenwich,
London, England, 2015

Encaenia Garden Party, Merton College,
Oxford, England, 2016

Hall Assistant Paul Whately, Christ Church,
Oxford, England, 2016

Brasenose College Ball,
Oxford, England, 2015

Christ's Hospital School,
West Sussex, England, 2010

Burns Night, St Hugh's College,
Oxford, England, 2016

Summer Eights, Oxford,
England, 2015

Following page:
25th Anniversary Ball, Kellogg
College, Oxford, England, 2015

Lord Mayor's Banquet, Old Bailey,
London, England, 2014

Pancake Race, the City of London,
London, England, 2014

Lord Mayor's Banquet, Old Bailey,
London, England, 2013

University Chancellor Lord Patten of Barnes
with his page, the Chancellor's Court,
Oxford, England, 2014

The Bedels, officiators at Oxford
University events, Oxford, England, 2015

Toasting the Queen, Swan Upping at
the Thames near Eton, England, 2015

'Trashing' after the final exam. This involves much foam-spraying, drinking and exploding bottles of champagne. Oxford, England, 2016

The Grecians' Ball with *Alice in Wonderland* theme, Christ's Hospital School, West Sussex, England, 2010

Ed Hills, head of Moreton House,
Harrow School, England, 2011

Ed Hills, head of Moreton House, having won the football match
against Druries House 2–0, Harrow School, England, 2011

BRITISH ABROAD
BESIDE THE SEASIDE

Travel, displacement, new surroundings and old colonialism: a series documenting
Britons and Britishness living abroad is collected here with a selection of photographs
that document the global tradition of an annual short escape away from home – the
summer holiday.

Vivian Smith, Fairlawn Hotel,
Kolkata, India, 2005

Nuwara Eliya,
Sri Lanka, 2005

Sam Levy's Village, Borrowdale,
Harare, Zimbabwe, 1995

Britfest, Schloss Neuhaus,
Paderborn, Germany, 2013

Borrowdale Racecourse,
Harare, Zimbabwe, 1995

The Kenya Derby,
Nairobi, Kenya, 2010

Singing 'Jerusalem' with Billy the Trumpet, England
vs Sri Lanka test match, Galle, Sri Lanka, 2018

The Karen Country Club,
Nairobi, Kenya, 2010

The Karen Country Club,
Nairobi, Kenya, 2010

The Royal Harare Golf Club,
Harare, Zimbabwe, 1995

Bad Fallingbostel army base, Heidekreis,
Lower Saxony, Germany, 2013

Kovalam, Kerala,
India, 2016

Clacton, Essex,
England, 2017

Following page: Last Day of Shravan,
Clacton, Essex, England, 2017

Nice, France,
2018

Miami Beach,
Florida, 2015

Following page: Grandé Beach,
Mar Del Plata, Argentina, 2014

Tenby, Wales,
2018

St Ives, Cornwall,
England, 2017

Sorrento,
Italy, 2014

Baga Beach, Goa,
India, 2018

PARRIFICATION AND THE PHOTO OBJECT

DAYANITA SINGH

In my eyes, the birth of photography is indelibly linked with the birth of the photobook: with photographic objects that can be held, collected and distributed. My history of photography starts with the English photo artist Anna Atkins' collection of cyanotypes, *Photographs of British Algae* (1843). Over the years following its first publication, she made 15 versions of the self-designed book, adding pages as the work grew. She did not sell the book, but found her own way of disseminating it among fellow botanists. For me, she is the mother of photography – she showed us what we could do with the medium.

Martin Parr has brought photography and the photobook to exactly where Atkins had begun to position it. Indeed, I believe that his positioning of the photobook is one of his greatest gifts to photography. He has published hundreds himself – particularly significant for me being the three-volume history of the photobook he created with Gerry Badger. That gesture alone has built a space for the photobook in the history of the medium, forever. He has also collected many thousands of others, his personal collection of 12,000 photobooks having been acquired by Tate in 2017 – a move that will help to build a foundation for this distinct form of photographic art to flourish.

What is key is that Martin's photography finds a place outside of the art gallery as well as within: in books, but also on objects, collectibles, postcards and ephemera. It is a space that is democratic and accessible. His books allow him to reach a more diverse audience than would be possible through exhibition alone, creating a closer dialogue between artist and reader – after all, this is not a single print on a wall, but images held together in a sequence authored by the photographer. Each book created by Martin has had his hand and thought in it – it is never just a collection of photographs.

For Martin, photographs are the raw material with which to build a story or an object that can facilitate a more intimate experience. The photograph isn't an end unto itself, but the beginning of a discussion, a provocation or reflection. He continues this by playing with the forms through which we view photography, taking it further than the book, onto clothing, packaging and commercial objects. Having already established that very distinct 'Parr' way of looking at the world – Parrification, as I call it – he is taking his Parr-branded world-view and flipping it on its head, creating a truly commercialized version of himself and of his photography. He whose work so often concerns the role of objects and possessions in expressing identity, creates his own.

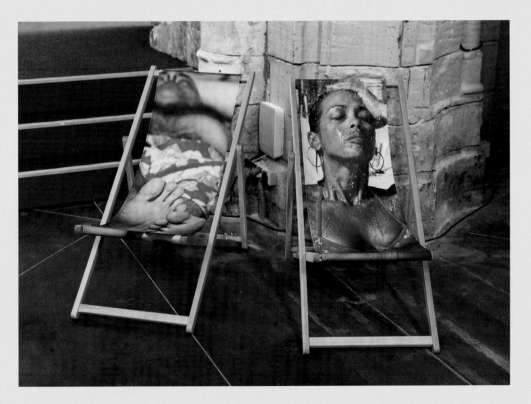

Paul Smith × Martin Parr
swimming shorts, 2017

Martin Parr deck
chairs, 2015

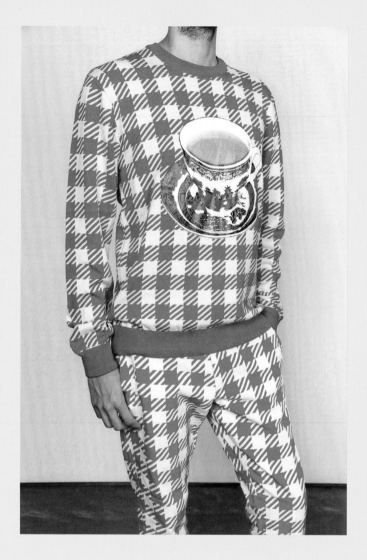

House of Holland × Martin Fucking Parr
gingham tracksuit, 2015

Lula Magazine × Martin Parr
washbag, 2014

Toiletpaper × Martin Parr
tote bag, 2017

Martin Parr beer mats by
Miniclick Photo Talks, 2016

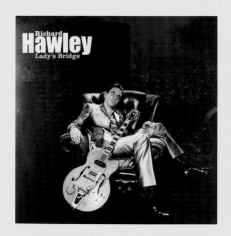

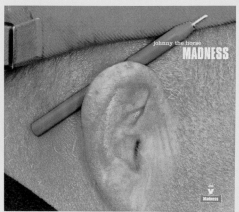

House of Holland × Martin Fucking Parr
seaside tracksuit, 2015

Lady's Bridge by
Richard Hawley, 2007

'Five Cuts' by
Madness, 1999

'Johnny the Horse' by
Madness, 1999

Autoportrait plate, 2010

Martin Parr limited edition
Bombay Sapphire, 2012

Martin Parr M&Ms, 2010

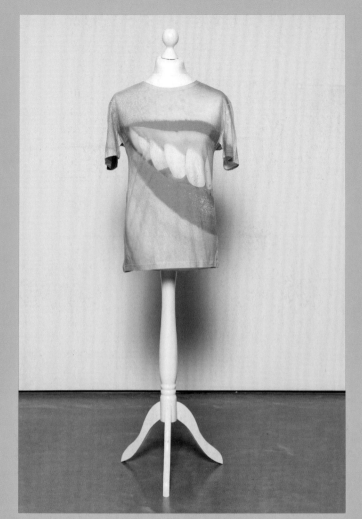

Martin Parr lipstick teeth
T-shirt, 2010

House of Holland × Martin
Fucking Parr scarf, 2015

Lula Magazine × Martin Parr
leather jacket, 2014

Toiletpaper × Martin Parr
scarf, 2018

SELECT BIBLIOGRAPHY

BOOKS BY MARTIN PARR

Bad Weather, A. Zwemmer Ltd, London, 1982, 297 × 210 mm, 96 pp, paperback, 56 photos, text by Michael Fish and Peter Turner

The Last Resort: Photographs of New Brighton (first edition), Promenade Press, Wallasey, 1986, 230 × 300 mm, 88 pp, paperback, 40 colour photos, text by Ian Walker; (second edition) Dewi Lewis Publishing, Stockport, 1998, 236 × 300 mm, 88 pp, hardback, 40 colour photos

The Cost of Living, Cornerhouse Publications, Manchester, 1989, 285 × 224 mm, 61 pp, paperback, 61 colour photos, text by Robert Chesshyre

Signs of the Times, Cornerhouse Publications, Manchester, 1992, 230 × 235 mm, 72 pp, paperback, 59 colour photos, text by Nicholas Barker

Home and Abroad, Jonathan Cape, London, 1993, 267 × 298 mm, 80 pp, hardback, 1 b/w photo and 58 colour photos, text by Ian McEwan; printed in paperback in 1993

Small World, Dewi Lewis Publishing, Stockport, 1995, 270 × 295 mm, 96 pp, hardback, 69 colour photos, text by Simon Winchester; published in French in 1995

Benidorm, Sprengal Museum, Hannover, 1999, 240 × 207 mm, 36 pp, paperback, 23 colour photos, text by Gerry Badger in English and German

Common Sense, Dewi Lewis Publishing, Stockport, 1999, 303 × 213 mm, 158 pp, paperback, 159 colour photographs

Autoportrait, Dewi Lewis Publishing, Stockport, 2000, 155 × 110 mm, 120 pp, hardback, 57 colour photos, text by Marvin Heiferman

Think of England, Phaidon Press, London, 2000, 270 × 190 mm, 128 pp, hardback; 133 colour photos; printed in paperback in 2004; published in French in 2000

Martin Parr, Phaidon Press, London, 2002, 250 × 290 mm, 356 pp, hardback, 156 b/w and 441 colour photos, text by Val Williams; published in French, German and Italian in 2002; printed in paperback in 2003

Martin Parr 55, Phaidon Press, London, 2007, 245 × 210 mm, 128 pp, hardback, 10 b/w and 46 colour photos, text by Sandra Phillips

Small World (revised edition), Dewi Lewis Publishing, Stockport, 2007, 245 × 300 mm, 96 pp, hardback, 74 colour photographs, text by Simon Winchester

Everybody Dance Now, Editions 2wice, New York, 2009, 292 × 212 mm, 96 pp, paperback, 8 b/w and 108 colour photos

The Last Resort (revised edition), Dewi Lewis Publishing, Stockport, 2009, 250 × 302 mm, 84 pp, hardback, 40 colour photos, text by Gerry Badger

Joachim Schmid is Martin Parr, Joachim Schmid/Blurb, 2009, 168 × 168 mm, 40 pp, hardback, 16 colour photos by Joachim Schmid, 16 colour photos by various photographers in the style of Martin Parr selected by Parr

Parr by Parr, Editions Textuel, Paris, 2010, 210 × 160 mm, 126 pp, paperback, 6 b/w and 50 colour photos, text by Quentin Bajac and Martin Parr in French; published in English in 2010, Schilt Publishing

A Book of King's, Third Millenium Information, London, 2010, 218 × 288 mm, 224 pp, hardback, 44 colour photos, edited by Karl Sabbagh

Life's a Beach, Aperture, New York and Editions Xavier Barral, Paris, 2013, 153 × 210 mm, 124 pp, hardback, 100 colour photos

The Non-Conformists, Aperture, New York, 2013, 238 × 203 mm, 168 pp, hardback, 90 b/w photos, text by Susie Parr

Martin Parr 55 (revised edition), Phaidon Press, London, 2013, 156 × 136 mm, 128 pp, 10 b/w and 46 colour photos, text by Sandra Phillips; published in French in 2013

Martin Parr (revised edition), Phaidon Press, London, 2014, 250 × 290 mm, 464 pp, hardback, 156 b/w and 441 colour photos, text by Val Williams

Black Country Stories, Dewi Lewis Publishing, Stockport, 2014, 315 × 230 mm, 140 pp, hardback, 105 colour photographs

We Love Britain, Schirmer/Mosel, Munich, 2014, 215 × 275 mm, 128 pp, paperback, 72 colour photographs, text by Inka Schube

Autoportrait (revised edition), Dewi Lewis Publishing, Stockport, 2015, 110 × 155 mm, 144 pp, hardback, 87 colour photographs

Real Food, Phaidon Press, London, 2016, 210 × 150 mm, 208 pp, hardback, 250 colour photos, text by Fergus Henderson

The Rhubarb Triangle, The Hepworth Wakefield, Wakefield, 2016, 222 × 286 mm, 84 pp, hardback, 40 colour photographs, text by Susie Parr

Remote Scottish Postboxes, RRB Photobooks, Bristol, 290 × 250 mm, 88 pp, hardback, 37 colour photos and 37 illustrations, text by Susie Parr

Oxford, Oxford University Press, Oxford, 2017, 315 × 230 mm, 224 pp, hardback, 118 colour photographs, text by Simon Winchester

Think of Scotland, Damiani, Bologna, 2017, 318 × 230 mm, 144 pp, hardback, 101 colour photographs

Small World (revised edition), Dewi Lewis Publishing, Stockport, 2018, 245 × 302 mm, 108 pp, hardback, 79 colour photographs, text by Simon Winchester

Beach Therapy, Damiani, Bologna, 2018, 305 × 222 mm, 102 pp, hardback

Martin Parr: Return to Manchester, Manchester Art Gallery, Manchester, 2018, 240 × 290 mm, 160 pp, hardback, 117 colour and 105 b/w photos, text by Martin Parr, Alitsair Hudson and Natasha Howes

BOOKS EDITED BY MARTIN PARR

Boring Postcards, Phaidon Press, London, 1999, 150 × 210 mm, 176 pp, hardback, 40 b/w and 124 colour postcard reproductions; published in paperback in 2004

Boring Postcards USA, Phaidon Press, London, 2000, 150 × 210 mm, 176 pp, hardback, 163 colour postcard reproductions

Langewilige Postkarten, Phaidon Press, London, 2001, 150 × 210 mm, 176 pp, hardback, 68 b/w and 90 colour postcard reproductions

The Photobook: A History Volume I (edited with Gerry Badger), Phaidon Press, London, 2004, 290 × 250 mm, 320 pp, hardback, numerous colour and b/w images; published in French in 2005

The Photobook: A History Volume II (edited with Gerry Badger), Phaidon Press, London, 2006, 290 × 250 mm, 320 pp, hardback, numerous b/w and colour images

Strangely Familiar, Peter Mitchell, Nazraeli Press, Portland, Oregon, 2013, 330 × 305 mm, 68 pp, hardback, 46 colour photos

The Photobook: A History Volume III (edited with Gerry Badger), Phaidon Press, London, 2014, 290 × 250 mm, 320 pp, hardback, numerous b/w and colour images

The Chinese Photobook (edited with Wassink Lundgren), Aperture, New York, 2016, 240 × 280 mm, 272 pp, 200 colour photographs

Strange and Familiar (edited with Alona Pardo), Prestel, New York, 2016, 240 × 280 mm, 272 pp, hardback, 200 colour photographs

INDEX

ACKNOWLEDGEMENTS

MARTIN PARR

My thanks go to Commissioning Editor Victoria Clarke, Project Editor Lucy Kingett, Managing Director James Booth-Clibborn, Publisher Deb Aaronson and CEO Keith Fox at Phaidon, to Melanie Mues for designing the book, to everyone at the National Portrait Gallery and of course to the Parrfighters and everyone at the Martin Parr Foundation.

It has been a great pleasure to work with Phillip Prodger, and I thank him for his insights, articulated so eloquently in his essays.

Many of the images included here have been commissioned by cultural or business organisations. I want to thank: Lavazza for sending me to the big tennis Grand Slams; BBC Creative for commissioning the ident group photos; Multistory, and in particular Emma Chetcuti, for the work in the Black Country; Aberdeen Art Gallery and Manchester Art Gallery; The Bodleian Library in Oxford; and the Guildhall Gallery in the City of London. Thanks also go to Magnum Photos for their continual support and the opportunities they have created.

Finally to Susie, who has tolerated my obsessive desire to keep on shooting over a period of 40 years.

PHILLIP PRODGER

I would like to thank Martin Parr for accepting the National Portrait Gallery's invitation to participate in this project, for making the free range of his archives available, for his generosity of spirit and for his support, advice and camaraderie. Working in collaboration with Martin has been a rare privilege. His remarkably efficient colleagues at the Martin Parr Foundation have also provided invaluable support, led by Foundation Director Jenni Smith, Head of Production Louis Little

and Studio Manager Charlotte King. The contributions of Nathan Vidler, Jon McCall, Mike Hale, Ashley O'Sheehan and Alex Parkyn-Smith are also gratefully acknowledged.

I am additionally grateful to colleagues at the National Portrait Gallery, led by Director Nicholas Cullinan and Director of Exhibitions and Collections, Sarah Tinsley. I also thank former Chief Curator Tarnya Cooper, her successor, Alison Smith, and photography curator Sabina Jaskot-Gill, who served as Coordinating Curator at the Gallery. In addition, I gratefully acknowledge the contributions of Rosie Wilson, Head of Exhibitions, Michelle Greaves, Exhibition Manager, Ben Weaver, Director of External Relations, Anna Starling, Head of Commercial, and Kara Green, Publishing Manager.

This handsome volume was produced by special arrangement with Phaidon Press. Working with Commissioning Editor Victoria Clarke and Project Editor Lucy Kingett has been an absolute joy. The book's wonderful design springs from the imagination and meticulous attention of Melanie Mues, whom I also thank sincerely.

I would also like to thank Grayson Perry, John Shuttleworth (aka Graham Fellows), Dayanita Singh and Joachim Schmid for their written contributions to this volume. In addition, I would like to express my gratitude to Jonathan Stephenson and his associates at Rocket Gallery, London, and Rose Shoshana at Rose Gallery – two of the most generous gallerists one could ever hope to meet.

I would like to thank my long-time collaborator Claudia Sorsby for advice on early drafts of the manuscript, and to acknowledge the inspiration of other authors who have written on Martin Parr,

including Val Williams and Gerry Badger. My special thanks as always to my wife April, who makes everything I do possible and my son Leo, who reminds me daily of the best bits of being human.

NICHOLAS CULLINAN, NATIONAL PORTRAIT GALLERY

We are enormously indebted to Martin for making this exhibition, and indeed this book, possible, and his collaboration and enthusiasm for the project have been stimulating. The exhibition began as a conversation between Martin and Phillip Prodger, then Head of Photographs at the National Portrait Gallery. Since that initial conversation, Phillip has conceived and led this fruitful collaboration. We are grateful to Phillip for doing such an outstanding job, both in curating the exhibition and in writing the essays for this book.

The guidance and assistance offered by all the Parrfighters at the Martin Parr Foundation has been invaluable and greatly appreciated: Tom Groves, Mike Hale, Charlotte King, Louis Little, Jon McCall, Jenni Smith and Nathan Vidler. Thanks also go to Jonathan Stephenson at Rocket Gallery and to Magnum Photos.

This beautiful book was expertly steered through the process by Victoria Clarke, Commissioning Editor at Phaidon, and Lucy Kingett, Project Editor, who have worked collaboratively with our gallery colleagues, in particular Ben Weaver, Director of External Relations, Anna Starling, Head of Commercial and Kara Green, Publishing Manager. Further thanks go to the Phaidon London team under Managing Director James Booth-Clibborn, including Imogen Blackwell, Graeme Eaves, Nat Foreman, Catalina Imizcoz, Koen Mastenbroek, Rebecca Price, Alenka Oblak and Inca Waddell, as well as to the book's designer Melanie Mues.

PICTURE CREDITS

We would also like to thank colleagues at the National Portrait Gallery for their hard work and dedication to this project, in particular those who have worked closely on the exhibition: Exhibitions Manager Michelle Greaves, Curator Sabina Jaskot-Gill, Director of Exhibitions and Collections Sarah Tinsley, Head of Exhibitions Rosie Wilson and Exhibitions Officer Claire Floyd. Numerous other colleagues at the Gallery have worked towards staging the exhibition, and I would like to express thanks to them all: Pim Baxter, James Cunninghame Graham, Andrea Easey, Nick Hanks, Andrew Horn, Jessica Litwin, Mark Lynch, Laura McKechan, Jude Simmons, Andrew Smith, Fiona Smith, Liz Smith, Denise Vogelsang and Helen Whiteoak.

This exhibition has been made possible by the generous support of Gucci. Their commitment has supported our ambition and vision for the exhibition and is greatly appreciated.

In addition, we would like to thank the Bern Schwartz Family Foundation for their significant contribution. The exhibition has also been made possible with the support of our Spring Season sponsor, Herbert Smith Freehills LLP.

Photographs © Martin Parr/Magnum Photos/Rocket Gallery, with additional credits listed below:

Courtesy Aberdeen Art Gallery: 152, 172b; Andreas Gursky © Andreas Gursky. Courtesy Sprüth Magers Berlin London/DACS 2018: 37b; Courtesy BBC: 56–67; Bert Hardy/Getty Images: 145tr; Bill Brandt © Bill Brandt Archive: 146t; Iris & B. Gerald Cantor Center for Visual Arts at Stanford University, Gift of Michael J. Levinthal/© Lee Friedlander, courtesy Fraenkel Gallery, San Francisco: 38tr; Collection Center for Creative Photography © Center for Creative Photography, The University of Arizona Foundation: 37tr; Courtesy DNB Media: 99; © Geoff Howard/National Portrait Gallery, London: 7; Courtesy Hans Eijkelboom: 37tl; Courtesy Lavazza: 108–109; Courtesy Manchester Art Gallery: 94, 160t, 170–171; Courtesy Royal Academy Silver Swans: 98; Courtesy Saskia Nelson, Hey Saturday: 23; Pictorial Press Ltd/Alamy Stock Photo: 146b; Courtesy Joachim Schmid: 19t.

John Shuttleworth lyrics reproduced by kind permission of Graham Fellows.

'Teeth' by Spike Milligan reproduced by kind permission of Spike Milligan Productions Ltd.

Phaidon Press Limited
Regent's Wharf
All Saints Street
London N1 9PA

Phaidon Press Inc.
65 Bleecker Street
New York, NY 10012

phaidon.com

First published 2019
© 2019 Phaidon Press Limited

ISBN 978 0 7148 7857 7
ISBN 978 0 7148 7858 4 (paperback edition)
ISBN 978 0 7148 7989 5 (signed edition)

A special limited edition of this book,
including a signed and numbered print
by Martin Parr, is also available. Please
contact the Publisher for information or
visit our website.

A CIP catalogue record for this book is
available from the British Library and the
Library of Congress.

Commissioning Editor: Victoria Clarke
Project Editor: Lucy Kingett
Production Controllers: Rebecca Price,
Alenka Oblak
Design: Melanie Mues, Mues Design

Printed in Slovenia

Published to accompany the exhibition
Only Human: Martin Parr
7 March–27 May 2019
National Portrait Gallery, London

The exhibition has been made possible
as a result of the Government Indemnity
Scheme. The National Portrait Gallery,
London, would like to thank HM
Government for providing indemnity and
the Department for Digital, Culture, Media
and Sport and Arts Council England for
arranging the indemnity.

Supported by Gucci

GUCCI

Supported by the Bern Schwartz
Family Foundation

THE BERN SCHWARTZ FAMILY FOUNDATION

Spring Season 2019 sponsored by
Herbert Smith Freehills LLP